Pagan Portals

Gods and Goddesses of Wales

A practical introduction to Welsh deities and their stories

Pagan Portals

Gods and Goddesses of Wales

A practical introduction to Welsh deities
and their stories

Halo Quin

Winchester, UK
Washington, USA

First published by Moon Books, 2019
Moon Books is an imprint of John Hunt Publishing Ltd., No. 3 East Street, Alresford
Hampshire SO24 9EE, UK
office1@jhpbooks.net
www.johnhuntpublishing.com
www.moon-books.net

For distributor details and how to order please visit the 'Ordering' section on our website.

ISBN: 978 1 78535 621 6
978 1 78535 622 3 (ebook)
Library of Congress Control Number: 2018940514

A CIP catalogue record for this book is available from the British Library.

Design: Stuart Davies

UK: Printed and bound by CPI Group (UK) Ltd, Croydon, CR0 4YY
US: Printed and bound by Thomson-Shore, 7300 West Joy Road, Dexter, MI 48130

We operate a distinctive and ethical publishing philosophy in
all areas of our business, from our global network of authors to
production and worldwide distribution.

Contents

Previous Titles

The Faery Heart (Lulu, 2011) ASIN: B00932SH6U

Pixie Kisses (Lulu, 2011) ISBN: 978-1447523444

Pagan Portals – Your Faery Magic (Moon Books, 2015) ISBN: 978-1785350764

Arawn! Keeper of the old ways,
Guardian of the gateways,
Master of the Cwn Annwn,
Hunter, magician, wild one!
Let us tread your paths with honour
Let us learn your ways with kindness
Let us be just and fair in your name!

This book is dedicated to the gods of Wales and the people who tell their stories.

Creoso y Gymru/Welcome to Wales

A kite wheels overhead, cries echoing on the hills. Geese lift loudly from the lake, and rabbits snuffle the grass. The land is lush and green, and the gods walk the fields and forests, the mountain tops and sea shore.

Here in Wales the legends are woven into the minds of the people. The schools teach the tales as part of Welsh culture, the theatres host reworkings and retellings of the myths every year, and the land itself is mapped in the stories. Steeped in the bardic tradition of this land, these gods and goddesses dance through the tales and hide their magic there. If you would find the old gods of this land, the Celtic gods of Britain, then the bards hold the keys to the otherworld.

This book is my offering to the land, to the gods, and to you. I hope that it will help you to delve, or dive deeper, into the stories which hold the keys to the magic of the land I adore, this place rich with magic and spirits, the gently-wild land of Wales. It is only an introduction, a leaping-off point for further work with the gods, spirits and stories themselves, but I pray it will be a strong introduction that takes you by the hand and guides you into the hills above the sea where you can discover the wonder of the gods for yourself.

There is no unbroken lineage for working with the Welsh gods, no book carried from pre-Christian times to this, but in the stories captured by medieval monks and carried from heart to tongue to heart again, in the buzzing of the bees and the blessing of the rains, we can find the threads which weave us home again.

Creoso y Gymru, land of the old gods dwelling in tales.

Chapter One

How to Use this Book

This book is designed as a starting point, not a comprehensive tome. I have laid it out in a linear journey, but you can skip between sections as they interest you.

I would be very surprised if you agree with everything I've included and I hope that you feel free to write your own correspondences and discoveries in the margins! Cross things out that don't work for you, add in pieces you find elsewhere, let this become YOUR reference book.

In Part One, we cover some notes on the Welsh stories, a brief introduction to the theory and practice of working with gods and goddesses in a neo-pagan context, and other useful contexts. Here are also suggestions for techniques such as altar building and making offerings to inspire you in using the information in each description of the gods.

In Part Two, we reach the encyclopaedic section with the gods. For each group of gods I've included a retelling of the main story they appear in, a description of how they can be encountered today, a list of key attributes, and some suggestions for things you might choose to represent the deity in question. The best way to get to know them is to get in touch with them and build your own relationship so this section gives a starting point for doing this. In 'Theory and Practice' you will also find suggestions for how to use the Visions for each god or goddess to meet the deities directly.

In Part Three, I've included some suggestions for going forward, for deepening your relationship with these beings, and a few closing words.

Part I

The Backdrop

Chapter Two

Sources, History and the Present Day

Sources: The Mabinogion

When people think of Celtic tales they often focus on the Irish myths, but Britain has another rich source of Celtic wisdom recorded in medieval times by monks in Wales, written in and about this land. My main source for the stories within is a collection of these tales known as the Mabinogion (Y Mabinogi, in Welsh). The Mabinogion is a selection of tales from medieval Welsh manuscripts, collected in both the White Book of Rhydderch (Llyfr Gwyn Rhydderch) and the Red Book of Hergest (Llyfr Coch Hergest), in the fourteenth century. While they are recorded in medieval times, there are indications that the stories within have older roots in an oral tradition, so we can explore them as gateways to the older, pagan gods of the land.

The four central stories in the Mabinogion which interweave are known collectively as the Four Branches. I've also included a little on some of the beings from the other tales in the collection, and the popular tale of Ceridwen and the Birth of Taliesin which is sometimes included.

I work from English translations of the text, but much of my understanding of it comes from listening to and telling the tales in the modern oral storytelling tradition. In spoken form the stories come to life. The versions of the tales in this book are, as a result, variations on the translations I have studied, influenced by my work with the beings in question.

The Mabinogion and Medieval perspectives

Many of the stories in the Mabinogion deal with challenging topics, including rape, murder, grief, loss, death, betrayal, war and more. They are set in medieval times and so the world in which we encounter the gods is patriarchal and formal. Blodeuwedd's story, for example, is particularly problematic from a feminist perspective; she is made for a man, given to him without consent, and punished when she chooses otherwise. Even here, though, we find patterns which make sense from a mythic context, layered underneath the surface.

We cannot know how these stories played out prior to the recording of them, and so it is worth keeping that in mind, but we can feel our way through the patterns and look for threads that might take us back. In all cases I have tried to look underneath the medieval veneer and our modern understanding to share some kernels which may help you find more about the beings within the tales. In this way I hope you will find useful keys to meeting the gods of Wales today.

It is possible that the stories were once very different, with clear illustrations of the beings as deities of the land, of sovereignty, of the turning seasons, and more. It is also possible that they were never like this. Regardless, today, we can find imagery, archetypes and energies which have taken many of us into relationships with powerful beings who, now if not before, bring us back to the land and the magic of life.

Modern pagan practice

Christianity came to these shores a great many years ago, converting the pagans of the land. Today there has been a modern resurgence of interest in non-Abrahamic religions of our ancestors embodied in the Neo-Pagan movement. Many people are finding a home in this movement, with its emphasis on relationship with the spiritual, a reverence of nature and a love of the tales which bring us home to the gods and the ancestors.

Much of neo-paganism is either heavily influenced by Wiccan practice, which in turn draws on ceremonial magic, or reconstructionist practices which attempt to recreate the practices of pre-Christian times. It need not be, however. There is a lot of space within neo-paganism for developing your own way of doing things, for finding what works for you and your community. None of these paths are better than the other, though respect, integrity and honour will carry you far in any of them.

My own practice is spirit-based, working through the stories to find direct contact, in order to build bridges between the worlds. I have studied Witchcraft, Druidry, Wicca, Core Shamanism, Heathenry, and other occult practices. As such, my personal practice would often be classified as eclectic but to the best of my ability I am guided by the magic of the land, the spirits and gods, and the stories in which they appear. I tell you this because it influences my approach but I also hope that this encourages you to find what works for you, rather than taking my words as gospel or as a reconstruction.

If in doubt, ask the gods, the ancestors and the spirits of the land!

Chapter Three

Theory and Practice

Theology: Gods vs Demi-god and apotheosis

Theology is a tricky topic. There is not a universally accepted definition of what a god is, for starters, or where they come from, or whether they even have an independent existence from the humans that talk about them! The beings written about herein, then, may or may not 'actually' be gods.

In most instances in this book the word 'god' has been used to keep things simple, but it is important to remember that there is no evidence that all the beings written about here were even considered to be gods when the tales found in the Mabinogion were written down. In fact, at the time they were written it was generally from a Christian perspective, so the divine or semi-divine status of beings may well have been played down. The line between divine and mortal is traditionally thinner than one might think in today's, (post-)monotheistic, culture, as can be seen in ancient Greek texts where there are cases of mortals becoming gods (a process known as apotheosis), and in Norse legends many of the gods will die in Ragnarok. Even if Rhiannon was not originally a goddess, today she is certainly approached as one in the neo-pagan community and thus perhaps she was once a mortal ancestor who has undergone apotheosis to take on a role which we call 'god'.

There are also different ways to cut the cake, so to speak. For example, Kristoffer Hughes describes the three categories of 'Magical Allies' as being:

Gods and Goddesses
Demigods/goddesses (half deity, half mortal)
Genius Loci, or spirits of place (including ancestors)

Whereas in the American Druid Fellowship (ADF) there are the three kindreds:

Shining Ones (gods, goddesses, and demigods – our elder kin)
Noble Ones (landspirits, Genius Loci, the Fair Folk and others of this ilk)
The Beloved Dead (ancestors, of blood, spirit, culture or choice)

This, then, might be something to consider when you approach the beings written about here. It might be that you are happy to relate to them as gods and leave the philosophising to others, if so that's great! Your relationship and practice is the most important matter at hand here. If it interests you to think about these things, however, here are some suggested questions to get you started:

What is a deity to you?

As you read the descriptions, would you classify these beings as 'gods', or as 'demigods', Ancestors, Faeries, or something else? Perhaps some of them fit under several categories (they certainly do in my work with them!) or perhaps you prefer not to classify them and to simply be with them.

How do you feel about the idea of apotheosis? Can a mortal reach divine status? Can a being become a god if they are treated as one? Or if they pass a certain challenge?

Is 'godhood' a part of the essence of a being, (like being physical, or red) or is it a role, like being a priestess, a father or an artist?

I have no answers to these questions, but part of the glory of a pagan path is that you get to find your own understanding of what works for you. (Including coming across and adopting a useful model developed by a tradition, or leaving the whole question in the realm of 'ultimately unknowable'!) The main thing to be aware of is that there is no clear evidence today that definitively labels these gods as deities, but there are plenty of practising pagans who have wonderful, supportive, deep relationships with them as such, and you can too.

There is also the ontological question of the way in which these beings exist; are they independent of us? Are they people in the way we are, or are they forces of nature which wear masks to appear like people? Are they even just psychological constructs, or archetypal forces of the collective Unconscious which speak to us? Ultimately we must navigate our own understanding of what exists, in every case including the nature of gods. My approach is that they have a reality in my life, which I feel very powerfully and which has a real, practical effect. That's enough reality for me!

Relationship & Devotion

In neo-pagan practice there are various ways to approach a deity, but all of them involve relationship. We can build relationship with the powers of the world and the beings of the land and the legends and, in doing so, allow ourselves to tap into the magic that they carry or embody. How, then, do we build relationship with gods?

The stories are quite clear on the importance of respect. The very first tale in the Mabinogion starts off with one Lord disrespecting another, and then having to make amends. We can take respect as a central tenet in building good relationships with spirits of any kinds. Without many records of how (or if) these beings were worshipped, we cannot reconstruct what our ancestors would have done. We can, however, draw on modern practices developed from anthropological studies, ceremonial techniques, and instinctive human behaviour to support our relationship building and, as long as respect for the gods and each other is kept in mind, we can't go too far wrong.

Any relationship must be based on knowing one another, so the first step is to read their stories, explore their lore, and come to understand a little about these gods in theory. In doing so, you may begin to notice their presence in your life; the song on the breeze with Gwydion's voice, the steadiness of Rhiannon in the hike along a path, the stars overhead wheeling with Arianrhod's magic. You may want to keep a note in a journal of things you notice which feel like it might be them moving through your life, feelings you have, pieces of lore or poetry or images that resonate with their power for you. In doing so you begin to get to know them in a way that is integrated into your life. This can be an act of devotion in itself, an offering to them to show them your sincerity and a gift to yourself which allows you to connect with the mysteries they embody and express.

Altars and Shrines

A traditional way of honouring gods and other spirits is by building a shrine (a devotional focus) or an altar (a space for magical workings). We do it naturally in collections of photos of family, fridge magnets which inspire us to joy that could be considered a shrine to delight, or in more obvious altars with statues or candles or bowls for making offerings. These can be very simple spaces with a single image or object representing the god in question, a picture hanging on the wall that reminds you of the landscape of Wales where they live, a single, scented plant, or complex Welsh dressers with shelves representing the different layers of the Welsh cosmos filled with statues and candles and objects for each deity and spirit you wish to connect to. There are some suggestions under each deity's section for representations connected to them which you can experiment with.

If there is a particular deity you wish to work with already, skip now to their section and consider their story and the list of correspondences and representations for them. What else might you add to this list? Clear a space, on a shelf, a windowsill, or even in a box of some kind, and collect an object or image or two that speaks to you of that god. This can be a good focal point for devotion, a place to read their tales, or somewhere to say prayers or do workings with them. Shrine building can be a little addictive, so you may find that you end up with every spare surface occupied by a god! Let it be something that evolves over time. These are never finished pieces but living homes for the gods and their mysteries to come to visit you and enter your life. You might like to think of your household shrines as guest bedrooms for the gods.

You can vary the kinds of altars you build for different senses and different locations. A box altar may be more suitable for your home, from which you can take items to set up temporarily, and then replace the items instead of leaving them out. You can use tactile objects for this such as feathers, thumbstones, and statues, or items such as a selection of small bottles containing perfumes or scents connected to the deities in question for you. A windchime or bells hung in a slightly drafty place will chime to remind you of them, and perfume diffusers are a safer permanent alternative to scented candles or incense if you want to leave it going permanently. You can keep hand-sized bells, singing bowls, rattles or small gongs on your altar in a small space for a sound-based interaction. You may have a specific song that you sing, or a specific album you play, when you light a candle, or hold a particular stone. You could also keep salt, spices, specific teas or similar according to how you feel they work with the gods you are building a relationship with. For Ceridwen in particular, for example, I like to brew and drink a cup of tea in her honour.

Altars are permanent or semi-permanent spaces in our lives which we set aside for connecting with non-physical beings, but what you keep in your space and how you interact with it will be completely personal to you.

Offerings and Prayer

If a shrine is like a guest room for the gods, offerings are the meals you put on for your guests and prayer is your conversation starter.

Once you have a space set up, what do you do with it? You might make an offering to the god in question such as incense, a glass of drink or a plate of food. These things are gifts from you to them and the energy of what is given feeds the spirits. Offerings are often given in the spirit of reciprocity – either to thank them for giving something useful to you, or in the hopes that they will do so in the future. Other reasons for offerings might include: to soothe a spirit that is being a nuisance, or to get them to leave, to strengthen them, as a gift out of love or a sense of duty, to mark a special occasion, or purely to reinforce a relationship. There are actions or objects included for each deity as suggestions to get you thinking about what you personally might offer the deity in question.

A time-honoured way to get to know a god is through prayer; speaking to them and listening to the responses. Prayers can be spoken, written, or thought, or expressed through dance, movement or other forms. Use the method of expression which is most comfortable for you. You might introduce yourself and ask to get to know them better, you might say thank you for something you feel they've already given you somehow, or you might ask for help with something in their domain. You might also offer up a praise prayer, where you just say how awesome they are, which is often considered to be a good offering. I've included prayers in the sections for the gods which you can use if they resonate with you, but it is often more meaningful if you speak from your heart or write your own words.

Listening may initially be trickier. We're often not encouraged to listen to disembodied beings so we've not necessarily developed the knack. You might find it easy, but if not, once you've said your prayer or made your offering relax and open yourself to feeling what kind of response they might be giving you. There might be an atmosphere, you might get a sense of a colour, a phrase, a scent, a symbol. Allow what comes to you to come, make a note of it and look at the patterns that emerge over time. You can also try divination such as tarot, runes or ogham, to receive the response through more tangible methods, or you can request a meeting in your dreams and write down what you dream of the following morning. Over time you will find a way that works for you and it will become much easier.

Pilgrimages

If you are lucky enough to live in Wales, or to be able to visit, there are places you can visit to bring you closer to the gods. The stories are tied to the land and most of the places mentioned in them can often be physically located. The energy and atmosphere of Wales is tangible, especially when you get away from the cities, and by visiting you can get a sense of the world that the legends are set in. The changeable weather, the rolling hills, the wildlife, the murmurations of Branwen's starlings, the greenery of Dyfed. All these things are still here and still hold the magic running through the Mabinogion.

A pilgrimage is a journey made with specific, religious or sacred intent. A journey done with the intention of bringing you closer to the gods and their home can have a profound effect on you and your understanding of them. Walking the land that they walked, breathing the air that tastes of the sea they knew and hearing the cry of the red kites overhead are all ways to build your relationship with them.

There are towns still thriving that they are said to have visited, there are standing stones named for them. You need not go far into the wild to meet the gods.

If a physical pilgrimage is impossible then you can also research images of the land, or recordings of traditional Welsh folk songs. The language has changed over the generations but it is still spoken in many places. You can even take courses to learn Welsh – though be aware that the language changes from area to area, so if you wish to use it on a future pilgrimage know whether you are studying Northern or Southern Welsh.

The Visions and the Stone

For each deity you will find a section entitled 'Vision'. I have given suggestions for an ideal location, but you may wish to sit at your altar if you have one, or in a comfortable seat in front of a table or similar surface where you can place a candle. Get comfortable, light a candle and begin with three deep breaths, allowing yourself to relax. Breathe steadily and deeply and allow yourself to sink into a meditative state; eyes half or fully closed. Then begin to chant the deity's name on a note that is comfortable for you, out loud if at all possible or in your mind if not.

Once you feel as though you are in a dreamlike, meditative state of mind, imagine the scene presented in the vision and allow it to play out like a dream or story. You may imagine it visually or have a sense of what is happening. You may hear the words spoken or simply get impressions. You may 'see' the deity as a person, or feel them as an energy, an atmosphere around you.

When the vision is over, make notes of anything that felt important about the meeting, anything you noticed, saw, felt, heard, and so on. Eat or do something physical to ground yourself back in daily life. You may wish to practise this process a few times or use a variation that is more familiar to you.

One practice you may find useful is to have an anchor stone. The name 'anchor stone' comes from the Order of Bards, Ovates and Druids, but this is a practice found in many traditions. A stone which can fit in your pocket is ideal, and if you can find one on a pilgrimage to a special site in Wales so much the better, but if not choose one that feels right. Whenever you sit down to meet one of the gods of Wales, whether using the visions offered herein or through prayer, or other practices, sit with your chosen stone in your hands and allow its weight to help you sink into your body and the here and now. Let it anchor you into the myths and cosmology of Wales. When you finish the vision, or your prayers, or whatever tuning into the gods you have done, feel the weight of the stone in your hand again, bringing you back into your body and the here and now. Over time this stone will build up a charge, magically and psychologically, so that just touching it will carry you into the right frame of mind and open the channels of communication between yourself and the Welsh gods. You may decide to have one stone for the whole pantheon, one for each family, or several, with individual stones for specific gods which you work with often. I would recommend starting with one to anchor you in the right frame of mind for connecting to the Welsh mythos and energies and seeing when it feels appropriate to expand your collection. You can also use stones set in jewellery, large pendants are good for this, so that it is easy to carry it with you during the day when you are building your connections. The connection is not in the stone; however, the stone is simply supporting your work.

Working with Almost-Lost Gods

Within these stories, and the other myths of Wales, we find both major and minor characters. For the most part these gods are not commonly worked with in a deep way although the work of Kristoffer Hughes, head of the Anglesea Druid Order, has begun to popularise them in recent years. Ceridwen is one exception, and Rhiannon, specifically in her role as love goddess, has a following in the Avalon Goddess Temple, created by Kathy Jones. For a long while these gods, if they were originally so, were almost lost to us, kept safe only hidden in stories and songs. What this means is that we have limited modern manifestations of people working with many of these gods and so it is often a very personal path to walk.

The best place to start is with what we do have; stories and a little archaeological work which can be used to compare the roles and characters of these gods to the Irish or mainland Celtic gods. To begin, then, spend time reading and listening to their stories. Explore writings about them and see how it makes you feel, what they inspire in you. Then spend time with them and allow an understanding of them to arise in your life.

Having a small role in the stories that have been recorded is not a sign that those with less written about them are unimportant, however, so if they call to you it is worth getting to know them. You may find yourself relying heavily on information which they give you directly, or which you interpret from the stories. In this case, hold it as a precious gift for your relationship and connection with them at this time. It may change and evolve but for now, this is true for how you relate to them and what they represent.

Something that is true for you or your group, but not found explicitly in the tales is often called 'Unverified Personal Gnosis' (UPG) and is valuable for you and your workings. It is best not to declare it as the 'Truth' in general unless many people independently share the same inspiration, or documented evidence is found that it was the case historically. Consider this to be a part of your personal relationship with them, just as you and a friend may have in-jokes or certain activities that you share with each other but not outside the friendship.

Build your altar. Make your pilgrimages. Write and say your prayers. Learn their stories and share them if you can. And see how the gods respond ...

Part II

The Gods

Chapter Four

The First Branch and the Gods of Annwn

Story: Pwyll's Descent

A long time ago in his court of Arbeth, Pwyll, Prince of Dyfed, heard the call to go hunting in Glyn Cuch. And hunting he went. Late in the day he became separated from his companions and, as the sun began to dip in the sky, he suddenly spotted a white stag, darting through the trees. Unearthly hounds were chasing it, their baying like a howling storm in the distance. He made chase and caught up with the hunt just as the hounds took the stag down, their white coats and red tipped ears flashing in the light. Pwyll called the hounds off and leapt from his horse to take the antlers for himself.

As his knife touched the still-warm fur, a shadow fell across the stag. Pwyll looked up to see a great, proud man on a dappled grey horse, wearing brown-grey hunting gear and a hunting horn.

'I know who you are,' said the huntsman, 'but I will not greet you as you have done me a dishonour.'

Pwyll, however, did not know who the huntsman was and could not see what dishonour there could be, but he was a good man and offered to make it right if he could.

The huntsman explained. 'I have never seen such a discourteous act as to drive another's hounds from their kill and steal it for their own.'

'I beg your pardon, but I am the lord of this land,' responded Pwyll, 'and so the stag belonged to me long before your hounds caught it.'

'In my land I am a crowned King in my own right. I am Arawn, king of Annwn.'

Now a king can pull rank on a lord regardless, but Annwn is the Otherworld of Wales and Pwyll knew now that the King before him not only had a higher rank than he, but was also much older, much more powerful, and had much more right to be hunting in the wildwood. Pwyll bowed deeply to Arawn.

Arawn set Pwyll a task to make things right; he must travel to the Otherworld to slay Hafgan, an otherworldly king who was terrorising Arawn's subjects.

'But how can I kill him?' Pwyll asked.

'Like so.' Arawn replied, 'I will make with you a strong bond of friendship. I will make you look like me, and I like you, so that no one will know the difference. In my guise you will rule Annwn, and the fairest lady you have ever seen will sleep with you each night in my chamber. A year from tonight Hafgan and I have sworn to meet by the ford. You must meet him there in my place and strike him just one mortal blow, and one blow only. When we fought last I struck him twice and the second healed him, now I can do him no damage at all.'

Pwyll agreed, for he wished to make things right, and Arawn showed him the way to his court. He cast a spell to make himself appear as Pwyll, and Pwyll appear as Arawn, and they returned to each other's lands.

Pwyll found that the Queen was indeed the fairest woman he had ever seen, and it was true that no-one saw through the magic of Arawn, so the whole court thought Pwyll was their lord, including the Queen. She was not only the fairest, but also the most down-to-earth, gracious and interesting lady he had ever had the opportunity to speak to. The moment they retired to bed, however, he turned his back and refused to speak to her or touch her, for he was not who she thought he was. Each day passed the same, and each night as well.

At the appointed time Pwyll went to meet Hafgan, and he struck just one mortal blow, as instructed.

'Ha, chieftain,' cried Hafgan, recognising that this, somehow, was not Arawn, 'What right do you have to kill me? I had no quarrel with you. But as you have begun my death, I ask you to finish me quickly.'

Pwyll lowered his head. 'I may repent for what I have done, but I will not slay you now.'

Hafgan was carried from the place to die and Pwyll sent out Arawn's people to gather oaths of allegiance from all the lords in the land. By midday the next day, the whole of Annwn was united under Arawn.

Pwyll met Arawn that evening as agreed and Arawn declared that Pwyll would always be a friend of Annwn. When he returned home to his wife she was surprised at the affection he showed her. It was then that Arawn truly knew what kind of man Pwyll was, and he told the Queen all that had happened.

Pwyll, in turn, found that Arawn had ruled so well that he had made the kingdom of Dyfed an even better place than it had been before. They became such good friends that they often visited with each other and exchanged gifts. Arawn and his wife named their new friend Pwyll Pen Annwn, which means Pwyll, Head of Annwn, and he became the custodian of a magical family of pigs who, no matter how often they were slain and eaten, would always be reborn to give meat again.

Arawn, King of Annwn

Arawn first appears as a huntsman, a man of the land, revealing his power as rooted in the earth. As huntsman he has a role in the cycles of life and death, and the magical Otherworld of Annwn can be seen as both the realm of Faerie and the realm of the Dead, placing Arawn as a god of the dead and the spirits. The gift of magical pigs that are reborn no matter how often they are killed and eaten reinforces this role. His hounds, the Cwn Annwn, are white with red tipped ears like faery animals, and so show Arawn's connection to the Wild Hunt which appears in many cultures as a host of spirits, often Fae. The Wild Hunt collects the souls of the dead, and sometimes hunts down those that have broken their oaths or committed other crimes. Just like Arawn, the Fae cannot abide dishonourable behaviour.

Arawn is not just a hunter; however, he is also a king. Arawn's mastery of glamour, a magic that makes one thing appear as another, puts him in the category of a faery enchanter and hints at the other magics he may hold. There is a lesson in Arawn's tale about appearances; we cannot know the whole story from one glance, a person is many layered and worthy of respect regardless of perceived hierarchies. Even the humblest of beings holds great value and deserves our respect and besides, one never knows how the gods will appear to us.

He rules Dyfed fairly, better, in fact, than Pwyll himself, demonstrating his fair and just nature. Arawn is Lord of the Wildwood, but he is not wild in a chaotic way, but in the way of life doing what he must, untamed. His powers show themselves in the growing of an oak towards the sun, the ivy covering the ground, the fox killing the hare and the soil's reclamation of the fox when it, in turn, dies.

Attributes and Symbols
Lord of the Otherworld
Ruler of Spirits, both Ancestral and Fae
Fairness and Justice
Cycles of Life
Keeper of Magic
Hunting
Valuing all beings, regardless of appearances
Cwn Annwn, the Hounds of the Otherworld
The White Stag

Ideas for Offerings
Go litter picking in a local piece of woodland. Leave birdseed for the birds in a wild place in his name.

Potential Representations
Hounds, stags, antlers, a hunting horn. Doorways to represent his ability to open gateways and allow entrance to the otherworld, so a rustic 'fairy door' would be suitable. Trees or forests. A mirror. The scent of the forest. The sound of a horn, hounds, or hunting songs.

Vision
Ideal Location: Woodland (if safe).

Name: Arawn

Close your eyes and imagine yourself in a clearing in the
   woods. As you chant the Cwn Annwn, with their red tipped
   ears and shining white fur, surround you protectively.
   The hounds are guides between the worlds, guardians
   and gatekeepers. The hounds settle at your feet and a tall
   figure appears, striding through the trees towards you.
   He is dressed in dark grey-brown hunting gear, a long
   hunting horn hanging from a strap across his body. He
   stops before you and the shadow of antlers branch from
   his head. Introduce yourself and listen to his advice. When
   it is time he turns to leave, his hounds follow and you are
   left where you were before. Note down his advice and be
   sure to follow it. Note too if he appears differently to you
   than described.

The Lady of Annwn

It is possible that once we knew the Lady's name, but it has been
lost to us now which tells us something important about her;
she is present in our lives but not always obvious. She is subtle,
supportive, holding space for the magic and following the flow
without forcing it. She forgives her husband and Pwyll for
their year-long deception, which shows great compassion and
understanding, but also suggests that she already knew what
was happening. The Lady seems to me to be the power of the
Otherworldly Land, the holder of the forces of what is.

Sweet Lady of Annwn,
Queen of the lands under the land,
Beating heart of the magical realm,
Lover, Lady, forgiving one.

By her actions she tests Pwyll, posing the question of how this
mortal man could prove that he is honourable, and not only

brave, or obedient to the instructions of Arawn, another Lord. It is common in legends that a hero will be challenged to accept a lover who appears ugly and wicked; here we have a hero challenged, without knowing, to not take advantage of someone who is vulnerable to deception. In this way she takes on a parallel role to Arawn who challenges Pwyll to be honourable in the social world, by challenging him to be honourable in ways that will have no foreseeable punishment.

Attributes and Symbols
Forgiveness
Acceptance
Steadfastness
Patience
Subtleness
Keeper of secrets
Challenger
Endurance

Ideas for Offerings
Tend or clear up a piece of land in her name. Plant a tree or
    sponsor the planting of one.

Potential Representations
Images of nature, trees, especially groves. A doe. Keys. The
    scent of a forest or wildflowers. Windchimes in the garden.

Vision
Ideal Location: Woodland or somewhere outside and
    overgrown.
Deity Name: Lady of Annwn (to be chanted softly)
Imagine yourself moving between trees in the woods. Ahead
    is a large tree with roots that form caves beneath. Enter the
    cave and descend into the earth along a sloping spiralling

passageway. The passage emerges in the courtyard of a castle and you enter through the doors. There she waits. Greet her and converse for a time. Perhaps she will tell you her side of the tale. Perhaps you will speak together of trust and honour, of forgiveness or endurance. Perhaps she will point out a challenge in your life that you need to face.

Listen carefully. When it is time to go, thank her and take your leave, returning across the courtyard, up the passageway and back through the trees the way you came.

Story: The Arrival of Rhiannon, Lady of the Otherworld

Once again, Pwyll Pen Annwn gets it into his head to have an adventure. Near his court in Arberth lies a magical mound named Gorsedd Arberth, where it is said that if one who is worthy sits upon it they will see a great wonder. If they are not worthy, however, they will receive three great blows. Pwyll and his retinue ascend the great mound and, at dawn, a white horse carrying a beautiful lady in gold and white silks emerges from the mists below the mound, walking slowly across the land. Pwyll is immediately taken with her and sends his page to bring the lady to him. The page sets off but no matter how fast he runs, he cannot catch up with the slow moving lady upon her horse. Soon she disappears from sight. The next morning Pwyll sits upon the mound again and, when she appears this time, he sends his fastest knight riding after the lady. Again, even though she seems to move as slowly as before, the horse and lady are gone before the knight can even get close. On the third morning Pwyll himself waits upon his fastest horse, ready as the sun crests the horizon. Again the lady emerges, walking so slowly across the land. Pwyll gives chase! Before he has even left the mound she is further than he thought possible, with every stride of his mount, her gentle walk carries her further out of reach until, as she reaches the morning mists at the edge of his sight, Pwyll cries out 'Lady! In the name of love, stop!' And she does.

When Pwyll reaches her side, his horse panting, hers serene, she turns to him and says, 'That would have gone much better for you and your horse if you had asked me sooner.'

It so transpired that this was Rhiannon, a noble Lady of the Otherworld, who was betrothed to a man she did not wish to marry. When Rhiannon heard of Pwyll she decided that he was the one for her and came to invite him to take her hand in marriage. How could he refuse?

First he travelled to her home and asked for the blessing of her father, Hefeydd the Old. A wedding feast was planned for a year and a day hence and he waited impatiently for the day to arrive. Arrive it did! The feast was magnificent, the drink flowed freely and there was food for everyone. Pwyll sat by Rhiannon's side at the head of the table and granted boons to all who asked in honour of the upcoming wedding. As the night drew to a close one last person came to the table, dressed in rags and covered in dirt asking for a boon. Before Rhiannon could say anything Pwyll had magnanimously declared:

'Anything you ask for, if it is within my power, I swear you shall have it!'

'Then I ask for the hand of the woman beside you for my own.'

The beggar cast off his rags and revealed himself to be Gwawl, son of Clud, the man Rhiannon had been betrothed to before. Pwyll could not be forsworn. Rhiannon thought fast and responded:

'What must be must be, but let my family and I have a year to plan you a wedding feast as grand as this one, it would not be fair to dishonour you with something less.'

And so it was that Pwyll returned to his home for a year and a day, without his bride once more. She had, however, given him a gift and a plan so that though Pwyll gave her away that night, she would never let Gwawl have her.

On the day of the feast Rhiannon sat at the head of the table with Gwawl and, as the evening went on he grew merry, but not so merry as to give away the lady he had claimed.

Pwyll left 100 soldiers waiting in the orchard and, dressed as

Gwawl had, disguised utterly, entered the hall and asked for a boon. 'If you have a reasonable request,' replied Gwawl, 'then I shall grant it.'

Pwyll held up the bag Rhiannon had given him and, as she had instructed asked only for enough food to fill the bag. Gwawl thought this reasonable and his attendants began to fill the bag. But no matter how much was placed within, it remained empty.

'Friend,'' said Gwawl, 'will your bag ever be full?'

'No,'' replied Pwyll, 'even if you put all you have into it, it will never be full, unless a true lord tamp it down with both his feet and say "sufficient has been put within".'

'Quickly brave sir!' said Rhiannon to Gwawl.

And so Gwawl did just that. Quick as a wink Pwyll pulled the neck of the bag over Gwawl's head and tied it tight. Then his soldiers entered the hall and one by one they kicked the bag as they passed it until Gwawl cried out for mercy from a dishonourable death in a bag. Hefeydd the Old agreed that it was unfitting and Pwyll asked for suggestions. Rhiannon then wisely gave her counsel:

'This is a fitting end to a story for minstrels and bards to tell, so if he releases his claim on me and mine and returns all to you that he took, and swears to never return, seek vengeance or lay a claim on anyone as a result of this, then let him out, and that will be punishment enough for him.'

Gwawl cried from the bag that he agreed and Pwyll released him. Hefeydd gathered more sureties from Gwawl and sent him on his way to heal. The wedding feast that had been interrupted a year before was continued and that night the union was consummated. The following day Pwyll and Rhiannon set off for Arberth together where they ruled well, side by side.

For the first two years of Rhiannon's rule in Dyfed, all was well. By the third year Pwyll's friends and advisers began to grow concerned that he was without heir and asked him to set her aside. He refused and within another year Rhiannon gave birth to a little prince. That night six women were placed over her and the boy to watch over them as they slept, but as midnight arrived each of the waiting women fell asleep too. They woke before Rhiannon to find the baby gone and, in an attempt to hide their failure to protect him they killed a puppy and smeared its blood on Rhiannon's face and hands. She awoke and, in horror, heard their accusations, begging them to be truthful, swearing she would protect them from harm if they were honest. They were too scared, and Rhiannon was from the Otherworld, so people believed she could behave in such a strange way as to eat her own baby.

Again, Pwyll's advisers told him to put her aside but he refused and, instead, Rhiannon was given penance. For seven years she would remain in the court at Arberth and each day she was to sit at the gate and offer to carry any new visitor on her back, like a horse, and tell them her story so that everyone would know of her shame, though few did let her carry them.

At that time the Lord of Gwent Is-Coed was Teyrnon Twryf Liant. He was a good man, with the best mare in the kingdom, who always foaled on May-eve. Somehow, however, the foal would always disappear so this year Teyrnon vowed to stay up all night and keep the foal safe. Early in the night the mare gave birth to a strong, handsome colt who could already stand unaided. Teyrnon was so surprised at its strength he commented aloud on it. Moments later a great monstrous clawed hand reached in through the window and grabbed the foal, dragging it towards the night! Teyrnon leapt up and cut the arm off at the elbow, hearing a great scream from the monster before giving chase.

It was so dark he could not see anything and he remembered that he had left the door open behind him, so he returned to protect the colt. In the doorway, to his surprise, he discovered a swaddled infant wrapped in a sheet of brocaded silk. He shut the door and carried the child to his wife. They had never been able to have children so she took him in as her own and her friends told others she had been with child all along. He was named Gwri Golden-hair, for his beautiful fair hair, and was nursed in their court. Before he was one year old he was larger than a three-year-old, before he was two he appeared as a six-year-old, and before the end of the fourth year he was grown enough to bargain with the grooms of the stables to help them with the horses.

Gwri's love of horses was well known and soon his mother suggested that the colt born the night he was found should be broken in and given to him. Together they made a fine pair!

Soon the story of Rhiannon's fate and the disappearance of her son reached their ears and Teyrnon realised that Gwri looked much like Pwyll, who he had known, and with a sense of honour but a heavy heart, for they loved the boy, they took Gwri to the court at Arberth and met Rhiannon at the gate where she offered to carry them, but each refused. At dinner that night, when Rhiannon returned from her post, Teyrnon told of what had happened and declared Gwri to be the lost son, and none there could disagree!

'If this is true,' Rhiannon cried, 'then I am delivered of my care at last!'

On hearing this, those there suggested the boy's name should henceforth be Pryderi, care, thus named by his mother when she first heard the good news of his return. His childhood name was set aside, and Teyrnon and his wife were ever cared for by Pwyll and, later, when he became the ruler of Dyfed, Pryderi himself.

Rhiannon, Queen of Dyfed

Rhiannon's name is often said to mean 'Great Queen' and her arrival on a magical white horse from her otherworld home suggests that she is, herself, otherworldly. As such she could be described as a Faery Queen. Despite the situations the world puts her in, Rhiannon consistently chooses to make her life better; twice avoiding an arranged marriage, for example. She is also kind, such as when she offers to protect her handmaidens from punishment rather than threatening them with it, or giving gifts to everyone who visits the court, even when they gossip against her. Rhiannon thus balances kindness with self-advancement, she is fair in her dealings with others, offers wise advice to Pwyll when he makes mistakes and remains calm and determined even during her own punishment.

Rhiannon is described in the story as being dressed in white, upon a white horse, but in many modern day encounters she is described as wearing red. Here we see the nature of the goddess as experienced by her followers today – she is both pure (white) and sensual (red), she can teach us about our own desires, and how to follow or pursue them with integrity.

Her arrival on a magical horse and her identification with a horse in her punishment (and her son's connection to the foal he grows up with), indicates her nature as a horse deity. Horses are partners to humanity throughout much of history. They give us their gift of travel, speed, stamina and power. With horses we can gain a vantage point to see further and plan better. So Rhiannon can help us see further, travel further, aspire further than we would alone. We can also call on her white horse to request help directly. Like Arawn, Rhiannon's abilities and behaviour, as well as the magical speed of her white horse, indicate her origin as otherworldly, beyond human, faery and divine.

In the Second Branch we hear of Rhiannon's birds, which are said to be able to sing the living to sleep and the dead to life. Perhaps you can tune into their power to help you with transitions, dreaming and magical journeying.

Attributes and Symbols
Queenship
The Horse
Faery Queen
Love
Strategy
Balance
Integrity
Challenges in Motherhood
Magical Journeys

Ideas for Offerings
Drop a friend or family member a note to remind them they

are loved. Donate to a horse charity. Send forgiveness and healing out to the world. Sing a happy song to the birds, or a lullaby.

Potential Representations

Horses. Songbirds. A heart. A crown. Birdsong. The sound of horses or drumming mimicking hoof beats. The scent of hay. Roses for love and thorns.

Vision

Ideal Location: Upon a hill with a view of the horizon.

Deity Name: Rhiannon

As you chant, imagine mists rising from the land around you. From the mist emerges a lady on a white horse. You begin to follow her but the faster you chase, the further she gets. Remember Pwyll's story and call out to her. She stops and waits for you. When you catch up she offers you a ride on her horse with her and she takes you on a short journey across the landscape, showing you things and telling you of their meaning for you in your life. Eventually you return to the place where you started. Thank her, descend from the horse and watch her disappear into the mists. Return to the place you began and as the mists fade you feel your body in the everyday world. Make note of anything important and ground yourself.

Pwyll, Penn Annwn

Pwyll is the being in the tales who comes closest to our own experience. He appears to have no magic of his own, performs no miracles, and belongs firmly in the land of Dyfed rather than the otherworld. He also makes mistakes, over and over again. What he does do, however, is move between the worlds. He listens and learns. His mistakes come from innocence, which is where all his actions are rooted. Pwyll acts from the heart until told how to do better, at which point he does do better. This shows great trust for which he is rewarded. He is a bridge-builder between people, a peace-maker. Pwyll played the role of Arawn in slaying Hafgan, and in doing so demonstrated that he is worthy of sovereignty, and he acted with courtesy towards the Lady of Annwn, showing his respect for her power. Although Pwyll is a ruler, he rules fairly, without dictation, listening to the advice of those whose wisdom he respects.

Pwyll may be a controversial choice for the title of god, but he has a lot to teach us, and through his actions became a lord of the otherworld, so deserves at least the same consideration as his Otherworldly wife Rhiannon. He is certainly one who can help us to meet the other gods.

Attributes and Symbols
The ability to listen and learn
Lord of Dyfed, Head of Annwn
Friend of the Otherworld
Innocence and trust
Respect and honour
Courage
The Crown
Thoughtfulness

Ideas for Offerings
Spend some time thinking about how you can make things right with someone, or support someone. If you can, do it. If you can do so without them knowing it was you, even better. A donation to an animal charity, even a small one, would be suitable for this.

Potential Representations
A crown. A stag, for his time as Arawn. A heart. A scent that reminds you to be thoughtful. A meditation bell.

Vision

Ideal Location: A castle or somewhere that makes you feel like a sovereign.

Deity Name: Pwyll

You find yourself in a throne room with a large open window looking out over the land of West Wales. Gazing out the window stands Pwyll, pondering a decision. Introduce yourself and spend some time with him. What does he tell you about his adventures? What does he tell you about innocence, trust, of leading without ego? What does he tell you about love?

When it is time for this meeting to end he may give you a gift or a piece of advice. Leave the throne room and return to your daily life. Note down his advice and anything else that feels important about this meeting.

Chapter Five

The Second Branch and the Protectors

Story: Brân and Branwen, a Tale of Heartbreak

The Giant, Brân the Blessed, a King of Britain, was visiting his court in Harlech with his brother, Manawydan ap Llŷr, and their half-brothers Nisien, who could make two warring chiefs find peace, and Efnisien, who could make two loving brothers find strife. From Southern Ireland they saw thirteen ships sailing towards them, one carrying king Matholwch seeking the hand of Brân's sister, Branwen, in marriage. Branwen was known as one of the Matriarchs of Britain, and the fairest maiden in the world but Matholwch also thought it would be good to unite the tribes of Ireland and the tribes of Britain in peace, and Brân agreed.

Branwen and Matholwch were wed at Aberffraw, though the feasting was held in a tent because Brân was too large to be contained within a house! Soon it was time for Matholwch and his people to leave and Efnisien came across the party as the horses were being prepared to leave. When he discovered that his sister had been given to someone without his consent or counsel, he maimed the horses horribly in retribution for the slight he felt. When Matholwch heard what had happened he was very puzzled that such an insult would be given to him after he was given such a wonderful woman as Branwen. There was nothing to be done in any case, so he and his men returned to their ships and to leave without saying farewell.

This, in turn, insulted Brân and his people, and so they sent a messenger to the ships before they could leave to find out why. In the end Brân made peace with Matholwch by replacing every maimed horse with a sound one, gifting Matholwch with a staff of silver and a plate of gold, and by explaining that it was his half-brother that committed the insult and so he could not properly punish Efnisien but that they should meet face to face to discuss what could be done. They met, and feasted again, and on seeing how much the loss of his horses and the attack on his honour had saddened him, Brân offered Matholwch a magical cauldron which could bring the dead placed within it back to life – though lacking the power of speech. At this, finally, everyone was satisfied.

Branwen and Matholwch journeyed together to Ireland and for a year Branwen was a gracious queen, giving gifts to any who came to visit. At the end of the year she gave birth to a son, an heir for Matholwch, who they named Gwern and fostered in the best place they could find. In the second year, however, people began to talk about the horses again, and they conspired to give Matholwch no peace until he had sent Branwen from their bed and locked her in the kitchen to cook for the court, and the butcher, each evening, would box her ear. Matholwch was worried that Brân would find out, so he stopped all ships from going to Wales, and any that came from Wales he had captured and imprisoned so they could not return.

Branwen was as smart as she was beautiful, however, and she lured a starling from the sky and over the next three years she gained its trust, taught it to speak, and told it all about her brother Brân. When it was ready she hid a letter underneath its wing and sent it across the ocean, where it gave her message to Brân. The moment he had finished reading, Brân mustered all his armies, set seven men to rule over the lands of Wales in his absence, and sent his ships across the sea to Ireland. Brân, however, was too big to ride on a ship, so he waded through the waters. When they drew near to Ireland, Matholwch's swineherds saw a forest and a mountain with a lake on either side of a great ridge, moving through the water. When they told Matholwch what they had seen he was puzzled and sent them to ask Branwen. She knew at once and told them so, the forest was a forest of ships, sailing, and the mountain was her brother, and the lakes were his eyes, dark with anger for what they had done to her.

The people of Ireland withdrew to the court and broke down a bridge between Brân and themselves, but Brân said; 'Let he who is head of his people, be a bridge for them also.' And so, he lay himself across the chasm as a bridge for his people to cross.

Messengers soon came to them on the road offering for Matholwch to step down and give the kingship to Gwern, although he was only five years old, as Brân's nephew. Brân told them he would rather take the kingship himself, so the messengers returned to Matholwch and asked for a better offer to take back to the invaders. Matholwch did not know what to do, and so asked for advice. Soon they had a plan, Brân had never encountered a house that could contain him, and so they would build one in his honour, and give Gwern Matholwch's kingship there to make peace. Branwen was asked to oversee the agreement and so she did, to keep the peace for the people.

The house was built. It was so huge that it had 100 pillars, and secretly, either side of every pillar were hung hide bags. And within each hide bag an armed man waited. Efnisien came into the house first and saw the hide bags. He asked one of the Irish men there what was in the bag.

'Flour, friend' was the reply.

Efnisien felt the bag, found the head of the man and squeezed until he felt his fingers sink into the brain beneath the bone. Then, he went to the next bag, and asked again. Again, he squeezed. Again, he felt the skull break. Again, he asked about the next bag, until he had crushed the skulls of all two hundred hidden soldiers. Only when that was done did he give the all clear for the waiting Brân and his men. Over the feast, peace was made, Gwern was made king, and everyone was satisfied. Little Gwern went to see Manawydan, Brân and Nisien in turn until Efnisien asked if Gwern would sit with him. Gwern went to his uncle. Efnisien, compelled but knowing it was a horrible thing to do in his heart, lifted Gwern by his feet and threw him directly into the fire. At that moment war broke out. Brân kept Branwen from following her son into the flames, and then from the fighting that raged around them.

Then Efnisien saw the Irish kindling a fire beneath the great cauldron of rebirth and placing their dead within it. Finally, when he realised that the fighting would continue until only the dead remained, he decided to make amends for the consequences of his actions and so he hid himself in the dead bodies until two Irishmen threw him into the cauldron by mistake. As soon as he was inside, Efnisien pushed outwards with such force that the cauldron burst into four pieces, and his heart burst also. In this way Brân's army prevailed, but only just. After all the fighting was done there remained only seven men, Branwen, and Brân himself who was wounded in his foot with a poisoned arrow.

Brân commanded that his head be struck from his body to be taken to Wales, and then London. And so, they did, and Brân's head remained alive and he continued to speak with them. On their return to Wales Branwen's heart broke for the hurt her life had caused the two countries, and she died. The seven survivors stopped for seven years in Harlech, with Brân's head and the birds of Rhiannon who sang to them. Next, they stopped for many years in Gwales, and as long as they kept the doors that faced Cornwall closed the head remained fresh and alive. Whilst there, their memories of the troubles they had seen seemed as a distant dream. Eventually they opened the door and their memories returned to them. Then, and only then, did they continue to London where they buried Brân's head facing across the sea. And there it stays under the tower of London, and so long as Brân keeps watch no plagues will come across to the lands he protects.

Brân fab Llŷr

Brân, Branwen and Manawydan are the children of Penarddun ('Chief Beauty') and Llŷr ('the Sea').

With his head buried under the Tower of London, Brân is a protector of Britain. He featured in the epic Welsh poem, 'The Battle of the Trees' disguised with an alder leaf on his shield. The alder does not rot under water and so its wood was often used to make bridges. Brân himself is a bridge for his people, serving and protecting them – even if the attempt goes badly in the end. He attempts to make peace at each stage of the Second Branch, even giving the Irish king a cauldron which makes his army undefeatable (almost) to make amends for the damage caused by his half-brother, Efnisien.

Brân means 'raven' and he is often known as Bendigeidfran, 'Brân the Blessed', or blessed Raven. Branwen, his sister, is often translated as 'white Raven', but '-wen' also means 'blessed' in feminine form, so the two are both blessed ravens, both carrying the same power, though expressed in different ways. The Raven is a very intelligent bird and often seen as a trickster figure, able to think outside of what is expected. Brân appears different to other men – he is a giant in life, and his head continues to live and speak after he dies – and Branwen teaches a starling to speak. Even with the efforts of the Irish king to stop communication, they find a way. Brân and Branwen, then, can be called upon to assist with communication in difficult circumstances. Brân is good at overcoming barriers in general, no house can contain him and no distance or chasm can stop him. Like the alder, Brân becomes a bridge to carry his followers across the treacherous distance.

Attributes and Symbols
Head/Chief
Vision/Farsight
Leadership
Self-sacrifice
Protector
Raven
Communication

Ideas for Offerings
Donate to a charity that helps ravens. Study ravens. Help someone get from one place to another. Compose a poem or song in honour of his deeds. Honour his sister. Plant an alder tree.

Potential Representations

Ravens. A bridge. A head. A shield. The Tower of London (under which his head is said to be buried). A giant. Alder trees. A raven feather. The sound of ravens cawing. A scent that makes you feel protective or protected.

Vision

Ideal Location: Outside with a view of the horizon.

Deity Name: Brân the Blessed, or Bendigeidfran.

As you chant Brân's name and relax, allow your eyes to close but keep the image of the horizon in your mind. In the distance you see the vast figure of Brân, as large as a mountain, moving swiftly towards you. As he gets closer, he becomes smaller, but still towers over you like a giant. He places his hand before you and invites you to step into his palm. You climb on and find a comfortable seat as he lifts you up to his eye level. Overhead there are ravens circling. The two of you speak, about journeys, about leadership, about listening, about caring for others. When it is time to return he places you back on the earth where you began. As you watch him stride back to the horizon and fade into the distance, feel yourself back in your body and open your eyes to the land around you.

Branwen ferch Llŷr

Branwen is described as the fairest maiden in Britain and so beauty is clearly one of her attributes, perhaps from her mother, Penarddun. Early on this beauty helps towards mitigating some of the damage done by Nissien as Matholwych cannot take offence in a straightforward manner when such a beautiful lady has been given to him. She also oversees the building of the house which is described as a peacekeeping offering and her marriage to Matholwych is, from the beginning, a way of forging alliances between potential rivals. Branwen is thus a peacemaker.

Just as Brân is the 'blessed raven', so too is Branwen. They share many qualities, especially skill at communication. Branwen's starling carries her words far across the water and land to gain help. Her voice is silenced and yet she finds a way to speak. If you feel silenced, and especially if you are endangered and need support to get help, Branwen is the goddess to call on. She continually seeks a peaceful resolution and is devastated by the death and destruction when things go wrong, so Branwen is unlikely to help with revenge or retribution, but healing and righting wrongs peacefully comes under her domain. Patience and endurance are also qualities she embodies.

Attributes and Symbols
Peacemaker
Beauty
Starlings
Communication
Patience
Endurance

Ideas for Offerings
Refrain from speaking for a day or set period of time in memory of her silence. Donate to a domestic abuse charity, or one for the homeless or refuges, especially women. Give away something beautiful. Take time to grieve the pain and loss in the world in her honour. Feed the birds. Honour her brother. Send a letter. Make amends.

Potential Representations
Starlings. Pictures of the murmurations (patterns that flocks of starlings make in the sky). A scroll. White ravens. An open cage. A sound or scent that feels like freedom after being trapped. The sound of starlings in the sky. A starling or white raven feather. A glass of salt water to represent

her grief.

Vision

Ideal Location: Under the open sky.

Deity Name: Branwen

Whisper her name, over and over. Allow yourself to relax and hear the beating of a thousand tiny wings. A flock of starlings swirl around you, hiding the world from view for a moment in a cloud of dark and shimmering wings. The starlings lift and in your mind's eye you watch the murmurations, the patterns they form in the sky. Allow impressions to arise. Are they making images, pictures, words? Are they communicating with you, or simply revelling in their freedom? As you watch the starlings above, you become aware of the lady Branwen walking towards you. Make note of how she appears, how she moves. She may simply join you and watch the starlings with you, or perhaps you start a conversation. Communication and connection can happen in many ways. After a while she hands you a scroll and turns to leave. What does the scroll tell you? The starlings descend and Branwen and the land are hidden. The beating of their wings fills your mind for a moment and the vision clears.

Chapter Six

The Third Branch and the Skilled Ones

Story: Manawydan ap Llŷr, the Master Maker

There was once a great battle which did not end well for anyone. Only seven survived to return home. After the dead were buried Manawydan turned to his friend, Pryderi, and admitted he could not return home to see his brother's throne empty. It was agreed that he would join the court of Pryderi in Arberth and marry Pryderi's mother, Rhiannon, with whom Manawydan would share rulership over a small area so they could settle down and enjoy the rest of their days in comfort.

They returned to Dyfed and Pryderi was pleased to see his wife, Cigfa, again. Manawydan and Rhiannon spoke, and enjoyed each other's company, so they both agreed to marry and were wed immediately. Together the four went to pay homage to Caswallawn, son of Beli, in England. On their return they feasted until they decided, that very night, to sit upon the mound on which Pwyll had first seen Rhiannon, Gorsedd Arberth. As soon as the four of them sat upon the mound with their company a mist fell and thunder rolled and suddenly, although it was night, there was light everywhere. When the mist and light cleared they looked around to see that no house or person, no beast of burden, nor even their companions was left, nothing except for the four of them and the empty buildings of Arberth court.

They returned to court and feasted, hunted, waited a while. They searched the land for their people but found no one, only wild animals. Eventually Manawydan declared they could not stay like that, so they decided to travel to England and seek a livelihood there. In Hereford they became saddle-makers, but they grew so skilled, so quickly, and the azure colour Manawydan painted the pommels – as he had learned from watching Llaser Llaes Gygnwyd – was so beautiful that the local saddlers lost all their business and conspired to kill the four of them. On hearing this Pryderi wanted to kill those that threatened them, but

Manawydan counselled against it and so they left Hereford and found another city where they taught themselves to make shields. Again their work was so skilful and swift that they drew the animosity of the local shield-makers. Again, rather than cause trouble by fighting they chose to leave and find another home. There they became shoemakers, thinking shoemakers of all people would not become violent. Manawydan made friends with the best producers of leather, the best goldsmiths, the best spinners. He learnt from the goldsmiths how to make gilded buckles and thus became known as one of the 'Three Gold Shoemakers'. He taught Pryderi to stitch so their work went quickly and their shoes and boots soon outshone any other.

Eventually this earned the ire of the shoemakers, as it had of the saddlers and shield-makers, and again they heard that their lives were endangered. Manawydan decided that staying in England was not working well for them, so they returned to Dyfed with supplies, where they gathered their hounds and hunted the land for a year.

One morning, while hunting, Manawydan and Pryderi came across a copse nearby which the dogs drew back from in fear. On closer inspection a great wild boar emerged and they gave chase, following it until it entered a lofty caer, a fort, which they had never seen before. The dogs pursued the boar inside and Manawydan and Pryderi waited for them to emerge. Time passed and the dogs did not return, there was no sound to be heard from the caer and Pryderi, against Manawydan's advice, entered the caer himself to retrieve his dogs. Inside he could see nothing except a marble fountain with a golden bowl upon it. Attached to the golden bowl were four chains which rose into the darkness above, seemingly suspended from the air itself. He was transfixed by the beauty and skill that he saw and he went to touch the bowl. No sooner had he laid both hands upon it but he could not move and could not speak.

Manawydan waited until near dusk, but neither Pryderi nor the dogs emerged so he returned home and told Rhiannon what had happened. Rhiannon immediately went out to find her son. She found the caer and she found her son, still as stone by the fountain. She could not free him so she laid her hands upon the bowl beside him. As soon as night fell fully a peal of thunder and a falling of mist came, and the caer vanished.

Cigfa was nervous about being alone with Manawydan, but he reassured her that he would continue to treat her as he always had, for both Pryderi's sake and her own. For a while they returned to England and Manawydan took up shoemaking again, but that went much as before so they returned to Dyfed with supplies and enough wheat to begin growing three fields full, for their hunting dogs were gone and they needed to eat. He grew the wheat and learned to fish and hunt and trap without dogs. The season came to a close and he resolved to begin the harvest the next day, as the field was golden with wheat. That morning he awoke to discover that every ear of grain had been sheared from the top of each stalk in the field. He checked over his second field and found that would be ready the following day and so resolved that it would be enough. The following day he found the same had happened again and so he checked his third field, and that had such beautiful wheat, ready to be cut. He returned home for his weapons and told Cigfa what had happened.

'I will keep watch and discover who is causing us such trouble once and for all.' He told her, and so, that night he hid by the field. Around midnight a mighty commotion arose and he saw the largest host of mice swarming over the field, one for each stalk of wheat, where they neatly cut the ear with their teeth and fled, carrying it with them. They were so fast and so many that, try as he might, he could not catch one, until he spied one which seemed heavier than the rest. She was pregnant and her weight had slowed her down enough that he could scoop her up in his glove. He carried her home and hung the glove on a nail above the fireplace, tied tight with string.

'What have you found?' Cigfa asked.

'A thief,' Manawydan replied, 'and I will hang her in the morning for her crimes.'

'It is only a mouse, surely it is beneath you to hang such a small creature?'

49

But Manawydan was determined and, at dawn, on Gorsedd Arberth he built a tiny gallows, crafted a tiny noose, and prepared to hang the mouse. It had been seven years since another human, besides the four of them, had been seen in Dyfed and yet, that morning, a clerk came up the hill to that very spot and asked Manawydan what he was doing. When he heard the clerk said:

'Surely it is undignified for a man of your rank to hang such a lowly creature! Let it go!'

'A thief it is and a thief it shall suffer the consequences of, as the law dictates.'

They argued a while but Manawydan would not be moved. The clerk offered him the money he had been given in alms in return for the creature, but Manawydan was determined. And the clerk went away.

Soon a priest came by, and much the same conversation was had. And again, Manawydan would not be shamed, not bribed into letting the mouse-thief go, even though the priest offered three times what the clerk had.

As the noose was strung about her neck a bishop arrived. He tried shaming Manawydan, he tried bribing him with a large sum. But Manawydan would not be moved. Soon the Bishop said:

'What would you take to set that creature free? Name your price!'

'That Rhiannon and Pryderi be freed.' Manawydan replied.

'You shall have that!'

'And that the charms and enchantments laid across Dyfed be lifted.'

'You shall have that too, now let the mouse go!'

'Not yet. Tell me, who is the mouse and how did she come here?'

'She is my wife and I am Llwyd son of Cil Coed. I cast the enchantments to avenge my friend, Gwawl son of Clud. And when they heard you were living here my warband asked to be transformed into mice to destroy your corn. On the first night they destroyed one croft, on the second the other. On the third night my wife and her ladies wanted to join them and, had she not been pregnant you would never have caught her. But since she is, and was caught, I will give you Rhiannon and Pryderi and free Dyfed from its enchantments. And now you know who she is, let her go!'

'No,' said Manawydan.

'What more can I give you?'

'That it is as if there had never been a spell upon the land of Dyfed, and none will be cast upon it, and that vengeance shall never be taken upon Rhiannon, Pryderi, or myself, for this.'

'Yes, yes. You are clever to say that or you would have born my vengeance later. As you ask, it will be so. '

And so Llwyd returned Rhiannon and Pryderi and lifted the enchantment upon the land, and Manawydan set the mouse free, who was returned to her human form. It transpired that during their time in Llwyd's court, Pryderi had carried the gate-hammers about his neck, and Rhiannon the collars of asses after they carried hay. But they were now returned to each other, their home and their people.

Manawydan fab Llŷr

Throughout both the second and third branches Manawydan displays his wisdom, first advising his brother Brân, then surviving the battles, and finally with his skill in crafting and patience with the local craftsmen, and the mouse-thief. Manawydan can be approached for advice in challenging situations.

His ability to learn new skills, and to figure them out from things he has seen, indicates a practical wisdom; an understanding of how things work, as well as skill in manifestation and following through on making things happen. He acts as judge when he encounters the magical thieves, but this is a demonstration of his ability to understand situations rather than necessarily about legal or moral judgment per se, evidenced by the suggested punishment being out of proportion for a mouse, and unnecessary for an act of nature. Seeing things for what they are, Manawydan acts from a place of knowing the truth in order to illuminate reality for others.

Manawydan can thus be approached for help with seeing the truth in a situation and understanding how to deal with it with wisdom. He can support the learning and use of practical skills performed to a high standard. He has the patience to allow him to act when the time is right, and the honour to not take advantage of the vulnerable, or blame others for understandable anger. These are things he can also support us with.

His name is said to reflect the Irish god of the sea, Mannanan Mac Lir, and Manawydan's father is Llŷr, which once meant 'sea', so his patience, wisdom (far-sight), and skill could be rooted in a seafaring past.

Attributes and Symbols
Craftsman
Skill
Perfection
Commitment
Perseverance
Seafaring
Observation
Honour

Ideas for Offerings
Make something with as much skill as you can and dedicate it to him. Perhaps it is a meal, or a drawing, perhaps you could put up a shelf. Do something with your hands in his honour. Study a useful subject. Help someone else with a topic you know well (if they ask for advice).

Potential Representations
Any good quality objects used in crafting. Shoes, saddles, buckles. A ship in a bottle would combine skill and represent Manawydan's likely roots. Objects that represent wisdom or skill to you. The sound of the sea. Sea-salt. Metallic scents. A pot of blue paint.

Vision

Ideal Location: an artist's studio or place of craft. On top of a hill. Docks by the sea may also be suitable.

Deity Name: Manawydan

As you chant, the world around you fades and you find yourself on top of a hill sitting beside Manawydan, looking out across the land. He is making something with his hands. Introduce yourself and ask if you can learn about what he is making and why. Perhaps it will illuminate something about your life, perhaps he will tell you something useful about creating objects or plans, or perhaps it is simply an interesting object and the reason will become clear later. You can ask him for advice or for help on a project. When you are ready, thank him for his company and help and let the vision fade.

Pryderi – Lord of Dyfed

The son of Pwyll and Rhiannon, Pryderi is the child of the union between the Otherworld (Annwn) and this world (Abred). First lost to the darkness, but found by Terynon when he saves his prize colt, Pryderi grows up as Gwri Golden Hair, brought up as the child of a nobleman and his wife who could not have children themselves. As Gwri, Pryderi is light in the darkness, hope in hard times. Eventually he is returned to his true parents and renamed, so in one sense he is born twice. His discovery alongside the rescue of the colt in the first branch, and the way he grows up with that colt, indicates a connection to horses which mirrors his mother's nature. Pryderi itself means 'trouble' or 'care', and the nature of his life is one of challenges. He is stolen away as a newborn, is one of the only seven survivors in the battles of the Second Branch, has all the people and creatures of his kingdom vanish and then, himself, is kidnapped by magic again. In the fourth branch we also see him lose the pigs of Annwn, and ultimately his life, to a magician's tricks.

In the third branch he and his wife Cigfa, Rhiannon, and Manawydan demonstrate great skills and Pryderi in particular shows an ability to learn quickly and well, akin to his manner of growing up. Pryderi can thus help you with anything that involves learning or studying, as well as having faith when you feel lost.

There is an argument that he and Pwyll are two sides of the same god. Both are connected to Annwn, Pwyll through his adventures in Arawn's court and Pryderi through his mother. Both end up as stewards of the Otherworldly pigs, and rule over Dyfed in their turn. Both their names refer to mental processes. In this case we might consider both Pryderi and his father as embodying ways of understanding and relating to the various worlds with care and thoughtfulness.

Attributes and Symbols
Child of Promise
Gwri Golden Hair – connections to Lleu
Challenges
Understanding others
Horses
Loss

Ideas for Offerings
Anything that helps horses, especially young ones. A donation to a charity for premature, newborn or orphaned babies. A candle lit in the darkness. Honey. An all-night vigil. A wish upon a star.

Potential Representations
Colts, gold, an empty bowl or container. Horse hair. Scents or music that help you concentrate. A meditation bell. A gold candle.

Vision

Ideal Location: Near stables or horses. (Taking sensible precautions if you are unfamiliar with large animals.)

Deity Name: Pryderi

Chant his name swiftly, so it has a rhythm like hooves striking the ground. Close your eyes and let the land shift around you into a meadow beside a dense forest. You can hear hoofbeats coming closer and soon a horse approaches with a laughing young rider, his golden hair shimmering in the sunshine. When he reaches you he may slide off the horse to join you on the ground, or he may invite you up for a ride across the land. Spend some time with Pryderi. Ask him to tell you his side of the stories. When the time comes to return, he brings you back to where you began and leaves. Gently return your focus to your body and the world around you and open your eyes.

Chapter Seven

The Fourth Branch, the Skies and the Seasons

Story: The Lady of the Flowers

*In North Wales there was once a Lord named Math ap Mathonwy who
had to keep his feet in the lap of a maiden except when he was at war or
he would die. For this role the maiden Goewin was employed. Math's
nephew, Gilfaethwy ap Dôn fell in love with Goewin and his brother,
Gwydion, noticed that he was pining away. Once Gwydion discovered
the truth he set about causing trouble, in order to lure Math away from
Goewin. As Gwydion and Gilfaethwy were Math's emissaries when
he could not leave the court, they were in the perfect position to do so.
Gwydion visited Math and told him of the pigs of Annwn which Pwyll
had been given by Arawn, King of Annwn and that Pryderi now kept.
Math wished to have some of these pigs for his court, and so Gwydion
said he would go to fetch them for him.*

*Gwydion and Gilfaethwy and ten men dressed as bards travelled to
Pryderi's court in Arberth. On arrival they were given food and drink
and asked for entertainment, which Gwydion provided for a great many
hours. Pryderi and his court were so pleased with Gwydion's works
that Gwydion convinced Pryderi that he could ask for help fulfilling
his errand, that of taking some of the pigs home.*

*Pryderi replied: 'I would gladly, except they were given to my father
under covenant and cannot be given or sold to another.'*

*'Well,' replied Gwydion, 'do not refuse tonight, but let me return
tomorrow with a proposition.'*

And Pryderi agreed.

*Away from the court that night Gwydion conjured twelve mighty
stallions, twelve perfect greyhounds, and collars, leashes, bridles and
saddles for each, all appearing to be made with gold instead of iron.*

He returned to the court the following day and said: 'You may not give me the pigs, nor sell them to me, but nothing was said about an exchange for something better.'

And he offered the twelve horses, twelve greyhounds, all their golden items, and even twelve golden shields conjured from a toadstool. Pryderi's court agreed that this was a fine plan and they gave Gwydion the swine in exchange for the fabulous beasts.

Gwydion and his companions left in haste for his spell would only last another day. They travelled fast but Pryderi's men discovered the trick and almost caught them. They built a sty for the swine in a town and hid them there, making their way quickly to Math's court. Math, of course, then needed to defend his home from the vast army that marched North.

On the first night that Math was away from his court, Gilfaethwy and Gwydion returned and, in Math's bed, Gilfaethwy raped Goewin.

A great series of battles ensued and many were killed. Eventually Pryderi sent word to Math calling for both sides to cease and for it to be fought only between Pryderi and Gwydion themselves. In this last fight Gwydion, through magic and strength, conquered and Pryderi was slain. His men went home without their lord.

Math and his army returned home and there Goewin told Math what had happened. He married her to make reparations for his nephew's behaviour and then punished both Gwydion and his brother by turning them first into a stag and a hind for a year, when they returned with a fawn which Math turned into a human and placed in fostering. Next he transformed the brothers into a boar and a sow, and after a year they returned with a piglet which was also placed into fostering. Finally he turned them into a wolf and a bitch, and they returned with a cub. Human again, penance paid and lesson learned, the two were then asked for their advice on who should replace Goewin.

Gwydion recommended their sister Arianrhod, daughter of Dôn, who was summoned to the court.

'Are you a maiden?' Math asked her.

'I know not but that I am.' Arianrhod replied.

'Step over my magic wand,' commanded Math, 'and we shall know the truth of it.'

And so she stepped over the wand. But with that step she dropped a young boy with rich yellow hair who let out a cry. Arianrhod ran for the door, dropping a small something else which Gwydion scooped up before anyone else could see and later hid in his chest at the foot of his bed. The boy was named Dylan and, the moment he could he made straight for the sea where he was completely at home.

Not long afterwards Gwydion heard a child's cry in his chest and discovered that the 'something' had grown into a boy. The boy was given to a wet nurse until he could come to court and live with Gwydion, which was not long because the boy grew fast. When he was four, he was already larger than an eight-year-old, he grew that fast. Soon Gwydion thought it wise to take the boy to meet his mother and so they visited Arianrhod's fort. When she greeted Gwydion she noticed the boy.

'And who is this, brother?' She asked.

'This is your son.' Gwydion replied.

'Why would you bring such shame into my home?'

'It will be no shame at all if I raise him well.'

'And what is his name, then?'

Gwydion could give no answer, for the boy had no name yet.

'Then,' said his mother, 'I shall place a destiny upon him that he shall have no name unless he gets it from me.' Gwydion could tell that Arianrhod had no intention of giving the boy a name.

They left and, the next day, Gwydion took the boy to the sea shore where he made a ship from magic and from seaweed he conjured leather in fine colours. On the ship the two travelled in disguise to the gate of Caer Arianrhod where they began to make shoes so fine that Arianrhod heard of them and came down to be measured for a pair herself. As Gwydion measured her feet, the boy saw a wren and killed it with a single throw of a stone from his sling.

'My, the fair one has a deft hand!' Arianrhod exclaimed.

And that is how the boy got his name; Lleu Llaw Gyffes, Fair One of the Deft Hand.

Gwydion revealed their true identity to his sister and she was furious at his trickery.

'Then I shall lay a second destiny upon him! He shall never bear arms unless I give them to him.'

Well, a boy cannot become a man without weapons, so this was a harsh one indeed. But they left and Gwydion hatched a plan. Disguised as bards they visited her fort again. Now, we already know that Gwydion is a good teller of tales, and this time was no different. In the morning they awoke with the sun to a great commotion; on the horizon a vast navy was approaching, ready to attack. Because the two had no weapons, being bards, Arianrhod gave them both some from her stores. The moment Lleu had his sword in hand Gwydion broke the enchantment and the approaching fleet disappeared. Arianrhod was more angry than she'd ever been.

'Then a final destiny I place upon the boy,' she cried, 'Never will he have a wife of any race on this earth.'

Gwydion couldn't solve this last riddle alone and so he visited his uncle, Math. Together they gathered flowers from oak, broom and meadowsweet and conjured a women made of flowers. She was the most beautiful maiden ever seen, and they named her Blodeuedd, Flowers. Blodeuedd and Lleu were married, and Gwydion procured a place from Math called Ardudwy, for them to live in.

One evening Lleu was on a trip to see Math when a hunting party arrived at Blodeuedd's door, led by a handsome lord, Gronw Pebyr, Lord of Penllyn. They were too far from home to return before dark so she invited Gronw in and they sat together that evening. Immediately they had fallen totally in love with each other and spent the night talking, and embracing. They spent three nights together and then she let him leave, fearing Lleu's return. Over the following year she conspired to discover how Lleu might be killed despite the magical protections placed upon him by Gwydion.

Firstly, it required a spear made over the course of the year and only when most people were at church on a Sunday. He could not be killed inside a house, nor outside, on horseback nor afoot, but only balanced on the edge of a river, under a shelter, with one foot on a bathtub and another on a goat. That was a position where he would be vulnerable to the spear made over a year of Sunday mornings.

When she had discovered this Blodeuedd told Gronw and he began to fashion the spear. As the year passed she convinced Lleu to show her just how impossible it would be to get into such a position by accident.

The day came that the spear was ready, the tub was prepared, the goat was found and the shelter constructed. Lleu climbed up into place and balanced as Gronw hid behind a rock, spear in hand. As soon as Lleu was where he needed to be, Gronw threw the spear which struck him in the thigh, leaving the head buried deep in Lleu who became an eagle and flew away. Gronw and Blodeuedd settled together into a happy life, deeply in love, in the home she had made.

When Math and Gwydion discovered what had happened, Gwydion set off to find Lleu. He searched everywhere until he heard of a sow who behaved very strangely, disappearing all day, and so he found the farm which kept the sow and convinced the swineherd to let him follow the swine the next morning. When the sow left the gate she ran so fast Gwydion almost lost her, but he kept track. Eventually he caught up with her under an oak tree, in whose branches sat an eagle with a great wound in his side, dropping rotting flesh which the sow eat from the ground with great glee. Gwydion sang a charm, known as an englyn, which called the eagle down to his lap, where he transformed Lleu back into a man and took him home to nurse him back to health and strength.

When Lleu was strong enough they returned to Ardudwy and Blodeuedd and her maidens ran away across the mountains. Gwydion gave chase. Her ladies were so scared they could not stop looking behind them and they fell into a lake and were drowned leaving Blodeuedd to be caught alone. As punishment Gwydion transformed her into an owl so that she could never see the sun again, and all the other birds would shun her. From then on she was known as Blodeuwedd, Flower-Face, which became another name for owls. Gronw hid in Penllyn, but Lleu found him and called him out. He declared it only right that he should get the chance to throw a spear at Gronw, for that was what Gronw *had done to him. Gronw countered that Lleu was known to be so skilled at throwing that that was somewhat unfair, so they agreed that a rock would be placed between them. Lleu threw the spear so hard, however, that it cut straight through the rock and pierced Gronw in the heart. And there the holed stone is standing still.*

Lleu returned to Ardudwy and ruled over it again, and the owl still cries at night for her lost love.

Arianrhod ferch Dôn

Arianrhod is queen of her own Caer (castle). She first appears in the story named as virgin – in the old sense this meant unmarried and whole unto herself. Math's staff shows that she has had sexual relations and thus is not a virgin in the modern sense, which is what is required for the job of footholder. The combination of these things indicates that Arianrhod is unmarried and owned by no man; she answers to no one and, without the magical interference of her uncle, would have had control over her own reproductive destiny.

Her anger at her son often confuses people, as he himself has done nothing wrong but she is said to 'curse' her son to never gain a name or arms except by her, and never to marry a human woman. The original word was not actually 'curse' but 'tynged', which is more of a destiny or fate bestowed upon him, similar to the Irish 'geas'. Each of these could be seen as ways in which she would have more connection to him than under normal circumstances, when he would likely have been fostered out anyway. As such, Arianrhod shows that she has a hand in the giving and shaping of destinies. Her name itself means 'silver wheel' and is often thought to refer to the wheel of stars (though many associate her with the moon as well). At the time the Mabinogion was written down there was knowledge of astrology in Britain and the influence of the zodiac, so perhaps as a star goddess Arianrhod was also showing her nature as a weaver of fate.

Caer Arianrhod was reached by sea and Gwydion's trickery often involves boats on the ocean. Her son Dylan was named for the waves and returned to it as soon as he was able, showing her nature as being connected to the ocean as a kind of mother of waves, at home in the sea, and so her connection to the moon as shaper of tides is suggested. Though Dylan is said to have become part of the waves, perhaps he did return to his mother. Where both Branwen and Rhiannon lose their sons, whether temporarily or not, Arianrhod has a hand in the upbringing of Lleu through the destinies she places upon him, and perhaps of Dylan.

Attributes and Symbols
Independence
Personal Sovereignty
Fate/Destiny
The ocean
Purity

Ideas for Offerings
Hand spun yarn or thread. Ocean water. Spin. Learn astrology and draw up a basic chart for someone. Learn astronomy and watch the stars.

Potential Representations
Stars, zodiac wheel, the moon, celestial bodies. Spindles or spinning wheels. Ocean imagery. Islands. Yarn or thread. Spinning tops. Scents that remind you of the stars or the sea. Seashells. Watermaker rattles.

Vision
Ideal Location: By the sea, a lake, or a body of water.
Deity Name: Arianrhod

Listen to (or imagine) the sound of the waves on the shore. As you wait at the edge of the water a boat comes to collect you and carry you to the island of Arianrhod. Let the waves rock you into relaxation. When you reach the island a path leads you up to a castle door which opens to welcome you into a throne room. Arianrhod awaits your visit. Greet her and introduce yourself. Perhaps she will tell you your destiny, written in the stars. Perhaps she will spin some transformational magic for you. Perhaps she will advise you in how to be more independent, if that is what you need. Perhaps you and her will simply talk a while. When it is time for you to leave, she bids you farewell and you return along the path to the boat on the water. It carries you across the waves and back to where you began your journey at the water's edge.

Blodeuwedd

Blodeuwedd begins life as flowers, as Blodeuedd (which literally means 'flowers' in Welsh). She is the beauty, passion and sensuality of the land made living. Math and Gwydion, two great magicians, transform her into a human shape, but she retains the magic of the land. An old tradition was that the king of the land gained his power from a marriage to the land herself and so Lleu gains not only a wife, but a claim to sovereignty through Blodeuwedd.

She, however, is not human and cannot be thought of as having the same social conditioning. As the sensual, sexual expression of the land she is more than a wife, so when she is given the possibility of a choice of lovers, she has no reason to choose the man she was given to. In fact, it could be said that this is a lesson in asking for consent; her consent is not requested so she cannot choose Lleu. And he suffers for it. Just as Arianrhod did not choose to give birth, Blodeuwedd did not choose to be married. In both instances they take matters into their own hands and do their best to change things. Unlike Arianrhod, however,

Blodeuwedd chooses only to change her own circumstances, although to do so Lleu must be removed from the land.

The dance of a goddess between two lovers is a motif found in many tales and is often seen as the relationship between the land and the seasons, specifically the dark and light halves of the year. It speaks to the changing of the land throughout the year, as well as the idea that sovereignty comes from the land, not from the person ruling; without her blessing, Lleu's sovereignty is revoked. Blodeuwedd can thus be seen as the goddess of the land, changing her face with the seasons.

Ultimately she herself is transformed into an owl. She goes from beings of sunlight to a creature of the night, flowers to owl. Again echoing her connection to the light and dark halves of life and her ability to connect to both of them. In both cases, she is wildness. Although being an owl is described as a punishment, she has in a sense returned to her original home outside of the human world, in the forest.

Blodeuwedd is a good goddess to contact if you want to learn to listen to the land and the voices of nature, if you need to become more comfortable living more fully in the light or the dark parts of yourself and your life, or to support you through unasked for transformations. She also knows very well the realms of sensuality, sexuality, wildness, freedom, consent, and knowing and following your own true desires. She can offer the perspective of the wild.

Attributes and Symbols
Lady of the Flowers
Magic of the land
Wildness
Freedom
Growth
Evolution
Choice

Turning the seasons
Marriage to the Land

Ideas for Offerings

Plant flowers in her honour. Donate to an owl sanctuary. Allow part of your garden to grow wild. Sing to the sun or the moon. Dance.

Potential Representations

Owls. Flowers, especially Meadowsweet, broom or oak flowers. Images of wildness or wilderness. Flower scents. Owl calls.

Vision

Ideal Location: At the edge of a forest at dusk.

Deity Name: Blodeuedd or Blodeuwedd

At the edge of a forest, as the sun begins to set, you see the flowers shimmer in the twilight. A beautiful young woman emerges from the trees. In the dim light her hair looks almost green and her eyes are dark as the midnight sky. Notice how she moves, how she appears. What mood is she moving with? Does she come to you as flowers made flesh, as Blodeuedd? Or is she an owl in human form, Blodeuwedd? Perhaps there are flowers or feathers in her hair. The gods often mirror ourselves back to us, so what does her appearance tell you about how you are in your life right now? Sit with her in the twilight, between the noonday sun and the midnight moon. Introduce yourself and perhaps she will tell you her story. Perhaps she will speak of the wildness in the land, or the magic of flowers. Perhaps she will teach you how to walk between the worlds, moving from light to dark. Perhaps she will remind you how to get in touch with your own desires, your own truths. Listen. Share your story with her. Twilight lasts a long time but, eventually, night falls fully. In the dark she shines with the light from deep in the earth. She takes her leave and the light fades. Return to where you began and open your eyes.

Gwydion fab Dôn

Throughout the story Gwydion looks for ways to help the people he cares about, albeit often at great expense to others: from starting a war to helping his brother, Gilfaethwy, assault the girl he desires, through creating a woman out of flowers to breaking his nephew's fate, (though his nephew almost dies as a result). Consequences aside, Gwydion always succeeds in what he sets out to do.

A master of illusion, Gwydion tricks an entire court into accepting toadstools and magic as a great gift of horses, greyhounds and weaponry. He also repeatedly disguises himself and his nephew in a way that tricks his sister, the boy's mother, in order to elicit a name and weapons from her, and finds the boy when he is hidden in a shape not his own. As such he is skilled in hiding and revealing truths and all matters dealing with illusion.

For causing a war which led to a great many deaths, and for attacking Goewin, Gwydion and his brother are punished by being transformed to live as a mated pair of beasts, forgetting who they are in the process. His behaviour following this punishment seems much more tempered, however, so we see that even a god can learn and grow wiser. His transformation of flowers into woman into owl as well as his own shapeshifting, gives him an understanding of what it is to live in different forms and this experience of having been forced to live as a gender that is not his own may give him an insight into trans and gender issues. Certainly his skills with illusion and revelation may help with transforming one's presentation and with bringing one's truth to light – or keeping it hidden if that is safer.

Gwydion is the master magician, although Math's magic may

be greater, Gwydion's freedom allows him to roam the land and grow as a magician over the course of the story. Magic is sometimes said to be the 'art of causing change in conformity with Will', paraphrased from the magician Aleister Crowley, and Gwydion certainly willfully causes change! Call on him, then, for any matters involving change, transformation, the revealing of truth or creation of illusions, presentation, manifestation of will, and development of magical skills.

Attributes and Symbols
The Magician
Transformation
Magic
Trickster-guide
Shapeshifting
Illusion

Ideas for Offerings
Optical illusions – acquire one on paper and burn it for him.
    Wear make-up or a mask in a manner unusual for you.
    Light a candle or a fire (make sure it is safely contained).
    Burn cinnamon or spices.

Potential Representations
A wand. Mirrors. Make-up and masks. Fire, as transformative.
    The magpie. Chanting. Singing bowls. Spicy scents.

Vision
Ideal Location: On a pathway, quiet road or track.
Deity Name: Gwydion.
As you chant, walk if you can, or imagine yourself travelling slowly down the track. Let the rhythm of your movement soothe your mind. From behind you come footsteps, Gwydion is travelling this road too. You wait and he catches

up with you, walking staff in hand. Introduce yourself and strike up a conversation as you travel together. Ask him where he is going, and where he would recommend a seeker of truths should go. Talk a while as you walk, you can ask for his help on something specific, or just share stories. Perhaps he will ask your perspective on something. Eventually the path forks and he says farewell and goes one way, while you turn around and return to where you began, allowing your everyday thoughts to return.

* * *

NB: Keeping focus on otherworldly beings whilst moving can take practice, but just allow yourself to relax and see what arises in your mind. Make sure it is safe to travel along the path you are taking as your attention will be split between the worlds. If in doubt, stop somewhere safe by the path instead of moving along it.

Math ap Mathonwy

Math is a king of Wales. His feet must remain in the lap of a maiden unless his court is at war, perhaps demonstrating that he must be totally in the state of war or the state of peace, but not between. He judges situations based on the information he has, and when he discovers an act of dishonour he works to balance the scales, by marrying Goewin after his nephews assaulted her, for example. Where Gwydion can change the appearance of people and things, Math changes their nature. Math is present when Blodeuedd is made from flowers, bringing the transformation of nature from wild land magic to human consciousness, and he transforms Gwydion and Gilfeathwy into creatures that forget their human nature and bear offspring together.

Math presides over order, justice and thus the categorisation of what is. He is Gwydion's uncle and apparent mentor in magic, perhaps holding the rules to an older form of magic which

Gwydion is still learning.

Attributes and Symbols
Transformation of type
Fundamental Change
Interconnectedness
Social Justice
Regulation/order
Magic

Ideas for Offerings
A white poppy for peace, a red poppy for battle. Mead, beer, or old drinks. Heat a small bowl of ice until it becomes water. File your tax return.

Potential Representations
A wand or staff. A throne or crown. Items representing legality or justice. Sandalwood or frankincense. A gavel (judge's ceremonial hammer – though these have never officially been used in Wales the sound and activity of rapping it might conjure a sense of the justice system for many in modern Western culture).

Vision
Ideal Location: A courtroom or throne-room.
Deity Name: Math
As the world around you fades you find yourself outside the door of Math's court. A soldier at the door grants you entry to the great hall where the king rests on his throne, his feet in the lap of a maiden and his wife Goewin seated beside him. His wand is laid across his lap. He invites you to step forward and state your case or question. Be sure you have one ready. Ask for his advice or opinion, if it is something you feel you have handled badly, you

can ask him for suggestions on how to make it right. You may find yourself speaking to Goewin as well. Allow the conversation to develop until it comes to an end and he sends you on your way, back through the door which is closed behind you. The vision fades and you are back where you began.

Lleu Llaw Gyffes

'The Fair-haired One with the Steady Hand' as his mother named him by accident. Lleu is often thought to have connections to the Irish Lugh, a god of sunlight and skill, and his fairness, steady hand, and similar name would bear this out. Some modern scholarship considers Lugh's name to be more related to contracts than to sunlight, and this also plays out in Lleu's tale. Lleu is born under strange circumstances and immediately taken under his uncle's care. Some say his uncle is therefore really his father, which could explain some of his mother's apparent animosity towards them for the situation. Between his uncle's care and his mother's involvement in his life through the tynghedau (destinies or taboos) she places upon him, Lleu is unusual in the world of the Mabinogion where most well-born children are put out for fostering and brought up far from their family.

Unlike the Irish Lugh, Lleu is not a particularly proactive figure in the stories; Gwydion solves the puzzles that Arianrhod places upon him, Blodeuwedd causes the changes in their home, and Gwydion rescues Lleu in the end. The most active things Lleu does is to throw a stone at a wren (which may have been part of Gwydion's plan), turn into an eagle to escape his death (though this may have been a consequence of the magic, rather than an act of Lleu) and throw a spear at Gronw, killing him, (though even this is in response to the spear thrown by Gronw earlier). If his mother is the wheel of fate written in the stars, perhaps Lleu is the follower of fate, like the sun that makes its daily path across the heavens.

Lleu has undeniable skill, focus and strength, however, and perhaps by the time the fourth branch ended he had learned some lessons, though what those lessons were we have not been told.

Attributes and Symbols
The eagle
Skill
Focus
Follower of Fate
Surrender
Destiny

Ideas for Offerings
Honey, as liquid sunshine. Burnt offerings. Light. Spend time perfecting a skill involving focus and throwing such as archery, juggling or javelin, or games of skill and luck like poker. Honour your teachers. Go sunbathing.

Potential Representations
Golden candles, depictions of the sun, the spear, eagles. Eagle feathers. Warmth. Honey. The sound of eagles calling overhead. Amber perfume or incense.

Vision
Ideal Location: In the sunshine.
Deity Name: Lleu
As you chant his name, allow your eyes to close and the world around you fade. You find yourself walking across fields of golden grain, towards a hill with a tall oak tree in full leaf upon it. The sun is high and bright and warm. Leaning against the tree is golden haired Lleu, sling tucked into his belt, spear by his side. He favours one leg over the other, weakened by his old injury. By his side is an old

sow, to which he is feeding acorns, and overhead an eagle is circling.

Lleu looks up as you approach and greets you warmly. You join him under the tree and he introduces you to the sow and gives you acorns from his pocket to feed to her. Spend some time talking to Lleu or relaxing together in the dappled shade of the oak. Lleu might tell you what happened when he returned home, or perhaps you talk about a skill you are trying to develop or improve. Allow the conversation to develop, ask him any questions you have, or just enjoy the company and note how you feel. Before you go, Lleu encourages you to soak up the sunlight as a blessing. When it is time to leave, say farewell and walk back down the hill and across the field to where you began and return to your everyday world.

Chapter Eight

The Hidden Tale and the Holders of Mystery

Story: Birth of Taliesin

Up in Snowdonia, upon the shores of Lake Bala, lived the lady Ceridwen and her two children. Her daughter Creirwy was beautiful and clever, but her son Afagddu was both ugly and so stupid that she feared he would never make his way in the world. She decided to use her magic to make him a potion to grant him the Awen, inspiration that would help him gain wisdom. She studied the books of the Druids and commissioned a great cauldron which was placed beside the lake in a hut where a fire could be kept burning beneath it. She enlisted the aid of the orphan, Gwion Bach, and his old, blind guardian Morda, to stir the pot and tend the fire for the year that it would take to make the potion. For a year and a day Gwion stirred the pot and Ceridwen gathered the herbs for the brew at the correct times, adding them with the correct words, waiting patiently for the magic to come to fruition. The day came when the brew was ready and Ceridwen went to fetch her son from the house. In those last few moments the potion bubbled, and the bubble burst, and the potion spat three drops containing all the magic of the cauldron onto little Gwion's thumb. He yelped from the burn and immediately, without thinking, put his thumb in his mouth to soothe the pain. At the moment the three drops slipped down his throat he became inspired. Gwion gained the knowledge meant for Afagddu, and he knew his life was in danger from the mother whose son had lost his way in the world.

Little Gwion ran. Behind him the potion left in the cauldron had turned to such dangerous poison that it cracked the cauldron and poured across the land, killing all in its path. When Ceridwen discovered what had happened she was furious and, seeing that Gwion had run, she gave chase.

He ran fast but she ran faster, so he took his new knowledge and transformed into a hare. Ceridwen became a greyhound and drew nearer. Gwion saw the river up ahead, so he leapt into the water as a salmon. Ceridwen became an otter and drew nearer still. Gwion leapt into the air and became a wren. Ceridwen followed as a falcon and plucked a feather from his tail. Finally, Gwion saw a farmyard below, littered with grains of wheat, so he curled up tight and became a grain, dropping to the ground. Ceridwen landed and became a great, black hen. One by one she ate every grain in the yard.

When she returned home as a woman once more, however, she found that the magic had transformed the seed of Gwion in her belly into a child. For nine months she carried him and when he was born she loved him. But the baby could not stay there, so she wrapped him in an oilskin and placed him on the ocean waves.

It was May eve and Prince Elfin, the unluckiest prince you ever did meet, was fishing from the weir. It was said that any who caught a salmon on that day would have good luck for the coming year and Elfin was determined to turn his luck around. Thus far he had caught a minnow, half a crab and an old boot. The sun was beginning to set when his line caught something large, heavy enough to be a great fish, and Elfin pulled it to shore! When he found only an oilskin bag he was not surprised. Unwrapping the contents, however, revealed something he had never expected to see, a baby that stood up, shining with a bright light, and speaking as eloquently as if he were fully grown.

'Prince Elfin,' the baby said, 'take me into your family and you will never again be unlucky, for I am the greatest bard that ever lived and I will turn your fortunes around.'

Elfin did not need telling twice, and so the baby was adopted and named for his shining brow, Taliesin. Sure enough, Taliesin did transform Elfin's fortunes from then on.

Ceridwen

Ceridwen sets out to help her children; she is a mother with magic, resources, drive and the knowledge to use it. As the mother of twins described as light and darkness, beauty and ugliness, cleverness and stupidity, she is the container of all possibilities, the cauldron of potential. Ceridwen knows where to go to get what she needs, from consulting the druids for the recipe for Awen, to hiring the blacksmith to make her cauldron, to enlisting the blind man and the child who will tend the potion while she is out gathering herbs for it. She cannot, however, see the future, or she would not have been surprised when the Awen went to Gwion instead of Afagddu.

Ceridwen is the one who creates the situation, then pushes Gwion into running therefore using his newfound knowledge and power for the first time, and finally rebirths him both from her own body and through the sea. She is the Initiator, the Transformative power which triggers change and growth. Her story is a lesson in patience and shows that gaining knowledge takes time, dedication and persistence. Her powers are symbolised by the cauldron in which the Awen brews as it is transformative, especially over time. The three different modes of transformation in the story show that change can come in different ways; a flash of inspiration, a long process of trying different things, or a deep introspection. Ceridwen's name is often translated as 'crooked white one', perhaps referring to the crescent moon which also transforms over time, bringing light in the darkness, or a silver sickle which reaps the magical harvest.

Call on Ceridwen when you need help finding inspiration in the darkness of your life, for learning about magic – though know that it requires patience – or being transformed. The journey through her cauldron, or being chased across the land, or feeling set adrift on the ocean, are not necessarily easy but they are life changing. A mother's love must be tough, sometimes. Even so, she is not always harsh and can hold even the darkest parts of us with kindness, like she cares for both her light and dark children. She can give you inspiration and show you the light that can guide you through the hard times, and she can wrap you in comforting darkness when you need to rest. Do not ask her about the future; ask her to help you through the present.

Attributes and Symbols
Magic
Wisdom
Inspiration
Initiation
Transformation
Dedication
Devotion
Motherhood
Learning/Teaching
Righteous anger

Ideas for Offerings
Tea brewed using herbs that you know have inspirational
   properties. Research magical plants. Cook soup or stew
   and dish up a portion for her and her children.

Potential Representations
Cauldron, book of magic, Greyhound, Otter, Falcon, Black
   Hen. The crescent moon. The Sow known as 'Hen Wen'
   (Old White/blessed). Herbal teas, freshly brewed or the
   dried leaves. The traditional English song called the 'Fith
   Fath Song'. ('Fith fath' means shapeshifting.) The smell of
   good food.

Vision
Ideal Location: In the kitchen.
Deity Name: Ceridwen
As you chant her name the world fades around you. You
   find yourself outside a cottage door. Knock and Ceridwen
   answers. Introduce yourself and she invites you in. The
   sound of a bubbling cauldron reaches your ears and you

feel the warmth of the hearth fire. Sitting at the large kitchen table you notice a teapot and cups waiting. Two children play on the other side of the room, one dark haired, one fair. Ceridwen gestures to you to pour the tea as she finishes stirring a cauldron of soup over the fire. She dishes up a bowl for you and a bowl for her. You eat together and she asks you what she can help you with. Perhaps you have a particular problem, perhaps you have something you'd like to learn. Perhaps you just want to hear about her story, her life, her children. Perhaps you just enjoy each other's company. When the soup and tea are finished and the conversation comes to an end, thank her and take your leave. She may give you a last piece of advice, or something to think about, or a herb to help you on your way as you leave the cottage. The door closes again behind you and you allow the cottage and landscape to fade, returning to where you began.

* * *

NB: Make a note of anything she gave you and research any herbs before taking them. They may not be safe to eat and instead have a different kind of lesson about how they grow, or their magical or mythological properties.

Taliesin

Taliesin, he of the Radiant Brow, reborn from Ceridwen's cauldron. Taliesin was an historical figure as well as a mythical one. The historical Taliesin wrote praise poems and sang for kings in the sixth century. He was known as 'Chief of the Bards' and some of the poetry ascribed to him can be found in the medieval Welsh Manuscript 'The Book of Taliesin'. The story of his flight from and rebirth through Ceridwen was recorded much later, but illustrates the myth of Taliesin, Taliesin as representative of divine archetypes and powers. Today Talisein is often called upon as a demi-god of inspiration, the bridge between the everyday and the Awen of the Bards. Perhaps this is an example of apotheosis in action.

As Gwion, Taliesin stirred the cauldron without tiring. He watched and waited and worked hard, but only doing as he was told. It was a matter of chance, or perhaps magical intervention, which granted him the bardic and magical powers to understand and become other beings, to express their natures through his own being, i.e. shapeshifting. By the time he reaches Elfin at the salmon weir, however, he has become reborn and takes on a more active role, offering his help to Elfin and the courts, speaking up and being seen.

Taliesin as an historical figure has left us with poetry we can read to experience the transmission of knowledge, language, inspiration through time. Taliesin as a divine being shows us the path which can lead to inspiration. Patience, studying a craft, time ... and then luck born of persistence. Luck, carried into the world through commitment – to not being caught, initially! This luck is given to the world through a self-knowledge and trust in one's abilities which can only come through surviving challenges, and through allowing inspiration to brew within our hearts and souls, as it must have while Taliesin floated on the ocean to his new foster-family.

Call on Taliesin to help you nurture the spark of Awen, to commit to the practice which makes the mind fertile for the seed of ideas, and then to tend the seeds as they grow. Call on Taliesin for confidence in expressing and sharing those creations you have grown and tended. Speak to him for guidance on how he overcame the challenges of transformation, as no rebirth is easy and life always brings things to endure or overcome. He has experience in these things, but, more than anything else, ask him if you need help with finding the right words, the right form of expression for what is necessary, for what is felt. He has his roots in poetry and, better than anything else, knows just which shape to take, or just which form to give an expression for it to get where it must go.

Attributes and Symbols
Initiation
Inspiration
The bard
Expression
Knowledge
Learning
Trust
Journeying

Ideas for Offerings
Write a praise poem or song honouring him. Study. Read or perform poetry. Light a white or golden candle. Take part in a poetry competition.

Potential Representations
Hare, Salmon, Wren, grain, a lit lantern, a quill pen. Ink. Spoken poetry. Scents which inspire.

Vision
Ideal Location: A feasting hall.
Deity Name: Taliesin
As you chant his name, a gentle mist full of golden light surrounds you and you can hear a voice singing. As the mist clears you find yourself in a busy court, tables heavy with food. Everyone is quiet, listening to the bard at the head of the room. As he reaches the end of his song, the room erupts into applause and you can see his performance is over. He leaves the great hall and someone comes up to you and beckons you to follow. They lead you to the room where Taliesin is drinking fresh water and catching

his breath. He welcomes you and you introduce yourself. He offers you food to share with him and you spend some time together. Perhaps you talk about the challenges you are facing, or perhaps he tells you about his time on the ocean, or what he learned watching Ceridwen brew her potion as he stirred. Perhaps he sings to you, or shows you his writings in progress, or takes you round the court when the meal is done. Perhaps you share some of your creations with him. Allow yourself time to enjoy his company. When it is time, he bids you farewell and hands you a token to remind you of your own powers of inspiration and craft. The person who brought you to his room leads you back to the main hall where you began. Taliesin steps onto the stage again and begins to sing. Mists full of golden light surround you and the hall fades from view until you find yourself, back where you began, in the here and now.

Chapter Nine

The Mabinogion and Beyond – The Others

Creirwy and Afagddu

Twins of light and darkness, opposites, potential,
recognizing and accepting what is

Creirwy and Afagddu are Ceridwen's children. In Hanes Taliesin, Afagddu (Utter Darkness) was a nickname for Morfran (Cormorant), showing his connection to the depths of the unknown, whereas Creirwy may mean 'Blessed Jewel', and shows her role as expression of light. The two children of Ceridwen embody the twin powers of manifest creation and are the driving force behind Ceridwen's quest for the Awen. In the tale Culhwch and Olwen, Morfran survives a great battle because his dark appearance makes those fighting think he is a demon which shows one way in which darkness can be a protection. Call on these twins to better understand the need for both light and darkness, and balance, in the world, and the source of inspiration, knowledge and magic. Tune into them individually to better understand their natures.

Dylan

The ocean, surrender, tides, cycles, seals and
sea creatures

Dylan is the son of Arianrhod, brother of Lleu, from the fourth branch. As soon as he is named (or baptised) Dylan leaves and takes on the nature of the ocean. I often see him as a young selkie-man, a shapeshifter that appears as a seal in the ocean, but he may appear differently to you. Call on Dylan to find your way to your true home and nature, or to get in touch with your deep emotional states.

Cigfa

Steadfastness, trust, skilfulness, preparation
Cigfa is Pryderi's wife, from the third branch of the Mabinogion. She travels with Pryderi, Manawydan and Rhiannon and helps with the crafting that earns them a living while Dyfed is under a curse. She remains behind when Rhiannon and Pryderi are taken to the otherworld, showing that she is of the human realm. Ask Cigfa for help with learning to trust and be patient.

Elfin

Changing luck, optimism, fortune, integration, practical support for divine work
Elfin is Taliesin's foster father, from Hanes Taliesin. He takes the great bard in and supports him in finding his way into wider society. In return, Taliesin looks after Elfin and his family. Get in touch with Elfin when your luck is bad or if you need practical help supporting your creative or spiritual work.

Gronw

Choice, love, sexuality, consent, changing seasons, the dark half of the year
Gronw is Blodeuwedd's chosen lover, from the fourth branch of the Mabinogi. Gronw arrives when Lleu leaves, leaves when Lleu returns, and throws the spear that results in Lleu's transformation into an eagle and may be considered in relation to Lleu as his darker twin. Gronw may help with transformations and uncovering your true desires.

Efnisien

Warbringer, trickster, chaos. Twinned with Peacemaker Nisien

Efnisien is Bran and Branwen's half brother, from the second branch of the Mabinogi. It is Efnisien who mutilates the Irish horses and triggers disputes, fighting and chaos. It is also, ultimately, Efnisien who sacrifices himself to put a stop to the battle, but the damage has already been done. Efnisien reminds us that actions have consequences and that insults, even in response to perceived slights, may not always be prudent. His twin brother, Nisien, never takes an active role but may be an indication that Efnisien is not all bad and that his actions come from attempts to make peace.

Teyrnon Twryf Lliant

Honour, Protection, Valour

In the first branch of the Mabinogi, Teyrnon rescues both his own colt and the child of Rhiannon and Pwyll from an otherworldly monster and raises the boy as his own, which hides the boy from further possible attack. As soon as he discovers the truth of the child's parentage he returns the prince and refuses reward, though Pryderi promises to keep Teyrnon and his wife as long as they live. Teyrnon can be called upon for help with protection and the defence of honour.

Gwyn Ap Nudd

Lord of the Otherworld, Hunter, Gatekeeper, psychopomp

Gwyn Ap Nudd, (White, son of Nudd) has strong connections with Glastonbury Tor as an entrance to the otherworld and is said to be the leader of the Wild Hunt, a host of otherworldly beings. He can be found in the Arthurian tale Culhwch and Olwen where he abducts Creiddylad, starting a war with Creiddylad's betrothed. Eventually the two men are set to fight over her every May Day, which has echoes with Blodeuwedd's story. Gwyn also helps hunt the great boar in the same tale and his role as a lord of Annwn and as a hunter suggests that he shares qualities with Arawn. Call on Gwyn for help with magical journeys or challenges.

Myrddin/Merlin

Magic, prophecy, skill, wisdom, mentoring
A great deal has been written on Merlin and he has several different forms. Merlin the Wild (*Myrddin Wyllt*) lives in the woods, driven mad by civilisation, Merlin the Advisor has integrated his understanding of the worlds of civilisation and the wild with his ability to prophecy to give him a unique perspective, and Merlin the Imprisoned was tricked by his lover and student Nimue, a Priestess, into being trapped within an oak tree. Ask Merlin when you need advice or an understanding of the future.

Elen of the Ways

Horned goddess, wayfinder, the threads of wisdom, reindeer
Elen of the Ways is described as an antlered goddess, and thus is connected to reindeer, their ability to migrate and find their way, their connection with magical flight – immortalised in Santa's flying reindeer – and thus both magic and travel. One of her manifestations is Saint Elen, for whom the Roman roads in Wales were said to be built and are named Sarn Helen, and who appears in 'The Dream of Macsen Wledig'. Elen can thus help with anything to do with travel, or with carrying knowledge and wisdom through the ages.

Modron and Mabon

Family, potential, archetypal forces

Mabon appears in Culhwch and Olwen, where one of the tasks set for Culhwch before he can win his beloved's hand is to rescue the lost Mabon ap Modron, whose name means 'Son, son of Mother'. Mabon is thus the archetypal child, and he reflects the tendency in the Mabinogion for children to be taken or lost as he was taken from his mother and imprisoned in a castle long before the tales were recorded. Modron is not seen herself, and so stands for all mothers. Call on their help for any matters dealing with family, and especially for healing the relationship between mothers and children.

Dôn

The land, ancestry, secrets of the stars

Dôn is the mother of Gwydion, Arianrhod and Gilfeathwy, and sister to Math. We know very little about her beyond this, except that the constellation Cassiopeia is known as the 'Court of Dôn' and her children often have features of the sky named as their homes, such as Caer Gwydion (Gwydion's Castle) being a Welsh name for the Milky Way. She is often considered to be a Mother-Earth Goddess figure, representative of the powers of the land, with her connection to the sky coming through her husband, Beli Mawr. Work with Dôn to understand the foundation from which all creativity, magic and transformation can occur.

Llŷr

The sea, ancestry, hidden depths

Llŷr is thought to be god of the sea, or the sea itself. Brân, Branwen and Manawyddan are his children, and Manawydan is also associated with the sea, though he may rule over activities associated with the sea, such as sailing, where Llŷr embodies the ocean itself. Work with Llŷr to understand the depths of emotions and interconnectedness of everything, as the sea connects all land.

Part III

Further Threads

Chapter Ten

Looking Forward

Once you have your altar dedicated to your deity, you've taken a pilgrimage to their land and spent time in meditation and prayer with them, what next?

Keep going.

This is the work of being in relationship with deity, prayer, offerings, honouring and remembering them. When you get stuck, ask them for help. When you are in need, pray to them. When things go well or your prayers are answered, thank them. When you notice their presence in your life, praise them.

As your relationship develops you will begin to notice when they touch your life, signs will appear that remind you of them. You might feel their guidance in a tug on your heart or in the song on the radio that plays after you pray. If you can, keep note of anything that seems particularly relevant or important so you can remind yourself later of what was said to you. This also gives you something to look back over for patterns and themes, which will show you more about their nature, and it means that on the occasions when you are having difficulties you can look back and remind yourself that you have felt their presence before.

Keep going.

Continue building and rebuilding your altars and shrines, write new prayers. Explore how they appear to you at different times of the day, the month, the year. See if they are closer in particular weather, or in particular places. Perhaps you'll notice that they grow distant at the dark moon but their voice gets stronger by the sea, or that you hear them most clearly in the forest at midday.

Different gods are more present in different circumstances, and different people are more sensitive to their presence at different times. You might struggle more in certain moods, or when tired, or you might become more open to them when you're about to sleep. Watch for patterns and use what you notice to build on your relationship.

Keep going.

In our culture we tend towards disbelief, so allow yourself to learn to trust what you are feeling, allow yourself to experience them as real, even if they are only real to you. Those experiences and interactions are important and have meaning and value in your life. Don't beat yourself up if you are struggling to think of them in the 'right way', or to feel their presence, or meditate every day, or anything. Build a relationship slowly. Start small. Allow yourself to remember them daily and just tune in, and let that be the foundation for everything else.

Explore what others have written, their history, stories, poetry and their culture. Let this inform how you connect with them, but above all, keep connecting.

Just keep going, and let the gods guide the way.

Author's Note: Happily Ever After

It is April Fool's Day today, a day for new ventures to leap, carefree, into the world. As I write this, the daffodils are in full bloom and the last of the lambs are appearing in the hills around my home. The tides of the Spring Equinox just passed turn the year towards summer. Blodeuedd blossoms in the spring flowers, Arawn hunts in the woodland, Branwen's voice echoes in the chatter of starlings over the edge of the ocean. The gods of Wales live in this place and I feel honoured, every day, to feel them in my life.

Every time we speak their names and tell their tales we open the way for the gods to come further into the world today. Every time we work with their stories and shed new light on them, we allow them to evolve and find more relevance in our lives. As we work with them, they work with us and we can all grow. In this way we become part of the family, part of the tribe of story-keepers who carry the magic and the blessings of the gods through time and space. You have now become part of this tribe. Take the stories and carry them with love. Face the shadows held within that you are ready to face, and hold the delights in your heart as a talisman against the troubles of the world.

Creating this book has been a journey in deepening my relationship with the gods of my home, and an offering to them and to you, dear reader. I hope you have found it useful in getting to know them and their stories, and that it will be a helpful companion on your path forward. Thank you for trusting me to travel with you a while, and may the bard in each of us, the sacred fool, be blessed with many 'happily ever afters'!

Diolch a bendition i chi,

~Halo x

1ˢ April, 2018

Halo Quin lives in the heart of West Wales where she studies philosophy, magic and storytelling, especially local fairytales and legends. She has written and published on pagan topics over the years, usually with a focus on working with the Fae; the spirits and the wild magic of the land, notably in *Pagan Portals – Your Faery Magic* (Moon Books, 2015). A lifelong practising faery witch, and a (more recent) member of the *Order of Bards, Ovates and Druids*, Halo offers divination, workshops, talks, and storytelling, and regularly runs seasonal rituals for the local community. Find more on her upcoming projects, adventures (and misadventures) at www.haloquin.net

Appendix I

Pronunciation Guide

In Welsh there are certain pairs of letters which make a single sound, and both 'w' and 'y' are vowels, alongside a, e, i, o and u, rather than consonants. Words can also mutate depending on the words and letters around them, and old Welsh had fewer letters covering a broader set of sounds than modern Welsh, so certain names can be spelled in a variety of ways. For example, b, p, v and f were once represented by a single letter, so 'Bran' can be found spelled as 'Bran', 'Vran' or 'Fran', though 'Bran' is most common today.

Vowels, a, e, i, o, u, w, and y, are generally pronounced as short sounds, unless they wear a circumflex, or 'little roof' (^), in which case they become long, or an acute accent (') which makes them shorter.

The stress on each word is almost always on the penultimate syllable.

'Eu' sounds like 'ay' as in 'hay'
'Aw' sounds like 'ow' as in 'sow' (a pig)
'F' sounds like 'v' as in 'vertical'
'W' sounds like 'woo' as in 'swoon', but is generally clipped
'We' sounds like 'wehh' which becomes 'we' as in 'web'
'C' is always hard, as in 'king'
'R' is trilled
'Y' is 'uh', as in 'huh', unless in the final syllable when it becomes 'ee' as is 'bee'
'Dd' sounds like 'thuh', as in a whole 'the' with a short 'e'
'G' is always hard, as in 'golf'
'U' sounds like 'eeh' as in 'eat', but can also be a clipped 'ee' sound as in 'hit'

'Rh' sounds like a soft breathy 'r' as in 'rhyme'

'Ch' is a soft 'ch', as in the Scottish 'loch'

'Ts' is a 'ch' as in 'church'

In Welsh a 'll' is a soft, hissing sound, created with the tongue placed gently on the roof of the mouth with a sustained exhale represented here by '*hl'

Afagddu (Av-agg-thee)

Annwn (Ann-oon)

Arawn (Arr-awnn – like 'around' without the 'd')

Arianrhod (A ree-ann-rhod)

Blodeuedd (Blod-ay-eth)

Blodeuwedd (Blod-ay-weth)

Brân (Bran)

Branwen (Bran-wen)

Ceridwen (Keh-rid-wen)

Cigfa (Kig-va)

Creirwy (Kray-rooi)

Dôn (Dorn)

Elfin (El-vinn)

Gronw (Gron-oo)

Gwawl (Goo-aool)

Gwri (Goo-ree)

Gwion Bach (Gwee-on BahCh)

Gwydion (Gwid-eeonn)

Harlech (Har-leCh)

Lleu Llaw Gyffes (Hlay Hlow Guff-vess)

Llŷr (hl-eer)

Manawydan (Man-ah-ooi-than)

Math (Math)

Matholwch (Math-ol-ooch)

Morda (Morr-dah)

Morfran (Morr-vran)

Myddin (Muhr-thin)

Nisien/Efnisien (Nee-Shenn/Ev-nee-shenn)

Penarddun (Pen-arr-thinn)

Pryderi (Pruh-deh-ree)

Pwyll (Poy-hl)

Rhiannon (Rhee-ann-on)

Taliesin (Tal-ee-eh-sin)

Teyrnon Twryf Lliant (Tay-nonn Toor-eev (second syllable is clipped, rhymes with 'give') Hlee-Ant)

Tynged/tynghedau (Tung-Edd / Tung-ehh-dhai)

Appendix II

The Houses of the Mabinogion

The four branches of the Mabinogion are often described as being about two clans, the House of Llŷr and the House of Dôn. In the first branch we meet Arawn, Pwyll and Rhiannon, who are not of either of the big families, but in the third branch their families are tied into the two main clans. Neither features in the stories directly, only appearing as the ancestors of the beings we meet. There are suggestions in other sources that their stories were known but have now been forgotten. You may wish to work with them and see what they wish to reveal to you about themselves.

* * *

In the first branch we journey to the Otherworld.

Arawn and his wife are in the Welsh Otherworld, Annwn, as is the rival king, Hafgan.

Pwyll is Lord of Dyfed and eventually marries Rhiannon, daughter of Heveydd the Old, also from the Otherworld. In killing Hafgan for Arawn he becomes known as Pwyll Penn Annwn (Pwyll, Head of Annwn).

Their son is named Pryderi, who marries Cigfa.

* * *

In the Second Branch we meet the House of Llŷr.

Brân, Branwen and Manawyddan are the children of Llŷr and Penarddun. Nisien and Efnisien are their half-brothers.

Later, Manawyddan marries Rhiannon.

* * *

In the Fourth Branch we meet the House of Dôn.

Dôn and Math are the children of Mathonwy.

Gwydion, Gilfaethwy and Arianrhod are the children of Dôn and Beli Mawr.

Lleu and Dylan are Arianrhod's sons.

Lleu marries Blodeuwedd, made by Gwydion, who later leaves him for Gronw, a neighbouring lord.

Penarddun is another of Dôn's children, and the mother of Brân, Branwen and Manawyddan, showing how both families are connected.

Glossary

Altar – a space for working magic or honouring a deity. Some altars are also shrines.

Shrine – a space containing representations of a deity in their honour.

Mabinogi, Y – A collection of Welsh stories recorded in the medieval period and compiled in the 12th–13th century, first published in full in both English and Welsh by Lady Charlotte Guest in the 1800s. Usually translated into English as 'The Mabinogion'.

Theology – theories of the divine.

Cosmology – a conceptual map of the way the world (or worlds) work in a particular culture or tradition.

Demi-gods – this comes from the idea that a being can be partly divine, or close to being a god. See the section in this book on 'Theory and Practice: Theology'.

Offerings – an object given, or an activity dedicated to, a deity, spirit or collection of beings.

Prayer – a communication directed at a deity or deities, often as a request, an expression of gratitude, or an offering of devotion.

Ground/Grounding (verb) – the action of coming back to normal consciousness, feeling back in your body and in an everyday mode of being after a trance or vision.

Vision – an imaginative experience which contains truth. In this book 'Visions' have been described as a structure through which the reader can imagine a meeting with a deity or being to get to know them better.

Anchor Stone – a stone or rock used to anchor the practitioner in a specific energy, mindset, trance state, or similar.

Otherworld – A world that lies alongside ours, operating on different rules even if it appears the same, which can be reached through certain magical means.

Annwn – The Otherworld, similar to the land of the dead or faeryland in some traditions.

Abred – This world.

Cwn Annwn – The Hounds of the Otherworld, Annwn.

Tynged/tynghedau – a spell which binds one to a certain fate, sometimes described as a 'curse', similar to the Irish 'geas'.

Fab/ap/ab/ferch – These are all words that are used in names to indicate 'child of', So 'Brân fab Llyr' means 'Brân, son of Llyr'. The three words are somewhat interchangeable based on the rules of mutations in the Welsh language.

Bibliography and Further Reading

Kristoffer Hughes, *The Book of Celtic Magic*, (Llewellyn Publications, 2017)

Kristoffer Hughes, *From the Cauldron Born*, (Llewellyn Publications, 2013)

Kathy Jones, *Priestess of Avalon, Priestess of the Goddess*, (Ariadne Publications, 2006)

Elen Sentier, *Shaman Pathways – Elen of the Ways*, (Moon Books, 2013)

Jhenah Telyndru, *Pagan Portals – Rhiannon*, (Moon Books, 2018)

Danu Forest, *Pagan Portals – Gwyn Ap Nudd*, (Moon Books, 2017)

R.J. Stewart, *The Way of Merlin: Prophet, the Goddess and the Land,* (Thoth Publications, 1991)

Lady Charlotte Guest, *The Mabinogion*, (Dover Publications, 2000)

Sorita D'Este (Editor), *The Faerie Queens*, (Avalonia Press, 2013)

J Williams ab Ithel & Iolo Morganwg, *Barddas*, (Red Wheel/Weiser, 2004)

Miranda Green, *Celtic Goddesses*, (British Museum Press, 1997)

Miranda Green, *The Gods of the Celts*, (Sutton Publishing, 2011)

Ancient Order of Druids in America, *Trilithon Vol II*, (Elphin Press, 2015)

J. Gwenogvryn Evans, 'Cad Goddeu/Battle of the Trees', *Poems from the Book of Taliesin*, (Forgotten Books, 2017)

Aleister Crowley, *Magick in Theory and Practice*, (Book Sales, 1992)

MOON

BOOKS

PAGANISM & SHAMANISM

What is Paganism? A religion, a spirituality, an alternative belief system, nature worship? You can find support for all these definitions (and many more) in dictionaries, encyclopaedias, and text books of religion, but subscribe to any one and the truth will evade you. Above all Paganism is a creative pursuit, an encounter with reality, an exploration of meaning and an expression of the soul. Druids, Heathens, Wiccans and others, all contribute their insights and literary riches to the Pagan tradition. Moon Books invites you to begin or to deepen your own encounter, right here, right now.

If you have enjoyed this book, why not tell other readers by posting a review on your preferred book site.

Medicine for the Soul
The Complete Book of Shamanic Healing
Ross Heaven
All you will ever need to know about shamanic healing and how to
become your own shaman...
Paperback: 978-1-78099-419-2 ebook: 978-1-78099-420-8

Shaman Pathways – The Druid Shaman
Exploring the Celtic Otherworld
Danu Forest
A practical guide to Celtic shamanism with exercises and
techniques as well as traditional lore for exploring the Celtic
Otherworld.
Paperback: 978-1-78099-615-8 ebook: 978-1-78099-616-5

Traditional Witchcraft for the Woods and Forests
A Witch's Guide to the Woodland with Guided Meditations and
Pathworking
Melusine Draco
A Witch's guide to walking alone in the woods, with guided
meditations and pathworking.
Paperback: 978-1-84694-803-9 ebook: 978-1-84694-804-6

Wild Earth, Wild Soul
A Manual for an Ecstatic Culture
Bill Pfeiffer
Imagine a nature-based culture so alive and so connected,
spreading like wildfire. This book is the first flame...
Paperback: 978-1-78099-187-0 ebook: 978-1-78099-188-7

Naming the Goddess
Trevor Greenfield
Naming the Goddess is written by over eighty adherents and scholars of Goddess and Goddess Spirituality.
Paperback: 978-1-78279-476-9 ebook: 978-1-78279-475-2

Shapeshifting into Higher Consciousness
Heal and Transform Yourself and Our World with Ancient Shamanic and Modern Methods
Llyn Roberts
Ancient and modern methods that you can use every day to transform yourself and make a positive difference in the world.
Paperback: 978-1-84694-843-5 ebook: 978-1-84694-844-2

Readers of ebooks can buy or view any of these bestsellers by clicking on the live link in the title. Most titles are published in paperback and as an ebook. Paperbacks are available in traditional bookshops. Both print and ebook formats are available online.

Find more titles and sign up to our readers' newsletter at http://www.johnhuntpublishing.com/paganism
Follow us on Facebook at https://www.facebook.com/MoonBooks
and Twitter at https://twitter.com/MoonBooksJHP